BĀRAHMĀSĀ IN INDIAN LITERATURES

BĀRAHMĀSĀ
IN INDIAN LITERATURES

Songs of the Twelve Months in Indo-Aryan Literatures

CHARLOTTE VAUDEVILLE

Forword by
T.N. Madan

MOTILAL BANARSIDASS
PUBLISHING HOUSE • DELHI
Email: naraina@mlbd.in • Website: www.mlbd.in
@mlbdofficial
+91 89 2999 9000

*Reprint: Delhi, **2024***

First Edition: Delhi, 1986

ISBN: 978-93-94201-99-6 (Hardcover)
ISBN: 978-93-5971-964-1 (Paperback)

Printed & Published by
Rajendra P Jain *for*
Motilal Banarsidass Publishing House
A-44, Naraina Industrial Area, Phase I,
New Delhi–110 028 (INDIA)
Email: naraina@mlbd.in Website: www.mlbd.in
Tel.: (+91-11)4751 1592
Delhi Showroom:
4637/20, F-2, Hari Sadan, First Floor, Ansari Road, Daryaganj
Delhi–110 002 (Opp. Fire Station) ***Tel.***: (+91-11)4559 7999
Bengaluru Showroom:
1st Floor, 1/2 Rathnavilas Road, Basvanagudi, Next to Pai Vista
Convention Hall, South End Circle Bengaluru - 560004 (India)

FOREWORD

The *bārahmāsā* is the song of the twelve months of the year and therefore of everyday life; the cognatic *caumāsā* is the song of the four months of the rainy season which revives life after the searing summer and produces among separated lovers the longing for reunion. These songs are a well-known and well-beloved component of folk culture all over north India, from Bengal in the east, to Gujarat in the west. They are simple rustic songs describing the cycle and moods of the seasons, but doing so in terms of deep personal feelings, whether these be associated with foods and drinks, the agricultural cycle, the observance of religious festivals, or the experience of the agonized longing of the wife for reunion with her lover-husband. If one listens to these songs carefully, with the bent ear, as it were, they may perhaps provide insights into the structure and significance of lived experience in the Indian setting.

Thus, the *bārahmāsā* (and *caumāsā*) may offer a clue to what is considered by many 'outsiders' a paradoxical aspect of Hindu culture : namely, the combination of an obsessive preoccupation with the flux of time—the almanac has been traditionally the most widely consulted guide to action in India—with a puzzling indifference to linear time as measured by clocks and recorded in historical calendars. As is well known, many western scholars have expressed dismay at what they consider the indifference of the Hindus (who are credited with some contributions to the cultural heritage of mankind) to the historical event—to exactitude in chronology. In everyday life today this indifference finds expression in a notorious disregard for the value of time. Punctuality proclaims modern man's willingness to submit himself to the control (even tyranny) of time as a key source of order in society given externally (socially or naturally). The watch that one wears on the wrist (or breast) is the magical gadget without which there will be chaos. But then it is also a manacle that-binds one in a manner the almanac never does.

Legend has it that the great Mughal emperor Akbar accepted the courtesies and most of the gifts presented to him by a couple of Catholic priests—the first Europeans he had met—on behalf of Portuguese merchants, but among the few things he rejected was a clock ! But who would say Akbar was not wise ? It would not be an exaggeration to say that for Indians generally the significance of time has traditionally lain in personal experience: what could be longer in duration than the separation from one's lover, or slower in coming than the next *kumbha* ? When it is so conceived time may not be measured by clocks but in diverse other ways, such as by calculating the movements of heavenly bodies, awaiting the predictably uncertain rains, or watching the ripening of golden grain. There are obviously many ways of reckoning time in human cultures, and the *bārahmāsā* is one such reckoner. In fact, it goes beyond mere reckoning : it makes time bearable.

I had heard the *bārahmāsā* mentioned, and had even listened to snatches of some songs, but the first scholarly discussion of this genre that I read was an article by Susan Wadley, a Syracuse University anthropologist (which later appeared in *Contributions to Indian Sociology* in 1983). Wadley had cited Charlotte Vaudeville's monograph *Bārahmāsā* (1965), and when Frederique Marglin, another anthropologist (from Smith College), mentioned it to me in 1982 as a work that ought to be translated into English, I was mentally prepared for the suggestion. I was able to discuss if with Professor Vaudeville herself, and she promised her cooperation, offering to re-translate the songs from the original Indian languages (Avadhi, Braj, Rajasthani, Gujarati, Marathi, Bengali) into English, rather than from the French translations prepared by her earlier. 'Translating from a translation', she said, 'yields poor results.' She did not have the time, however, to write a new introduction or translate the old one. The help of a professional translator was required for this purpose and I turned to Mr. Clemens Heller, Administreteur adjoint, Foundation de La Maison des Sciences de l'Homme. His response was characteristically generous. Thus assured of a text, I approached for Mr. Narendra Prakash Jain (of Motilal Banarsidass, the well-known publishers of indological works), and he agreed to undertake the production and publication of the book. Subsequently, Professor Vaudeville entrusted the translation of the introductory essay to Ms. Heather Willings who prepared it in consultation with the author. It is a pleasure to record here the cooperation of all these persons in making it possible to bring out this English edition of *bārahmāsā* which should have a wide readership in India and abroad.

My task as the writer of the Foreword is done. I will not be so presumptuous as to suggest that the distinguished author of this monograph, Professor Charlotte Vaudeville (who is a familiar, friendly and esteemed colleague of Indianists, not only in Paris, where she is a professor at the Ecole Pratique des Hautes Etudes, but also in such far-flung places of learning as Banaras Hindu University, Cambridge University, Chicago University, Harvard University, Poona University, and the University of California at Berkeley) needs any introduction. It is a pleasure, however, to acknowledge here the indebtedness of Indians and Indianists to her for her monumental work on Kabir and for her other numerous publications based on Indian folklore and vernacular literatures of modern India.

Institute of Economic Growth, Delhi T. N. MADAN
30 April 1986

PREFACE

The present book is a revised and somewhat enlarged English version of a work first written in French and published in 1965.[1] My first work on the "Bārahmāsā" genre was born from a growing awareness of the extraordinary richness and intrinsic value of the folk-songs composed in various Indo-Aryan vernaculars, some of which did not even have any written literature to boast about. The early Western Indologists, on the whole, were mostly attracted to the ancient literatures of India, composed in Sanskrit or Prakrit, which were the vehicle of the so-called "Great Tradition". Folk literature as a whole, especially village songs, remained beyond the pale as far as Indology was concerned. Such was also the case with Indian scholars trained in the methods of Western scholarship.

The first attempt at editing and translating some Indian village songs was made in 1871 by C. E. GROVER* who preceded by a few years the great Linguist and Indologist George GRIERSON, whose *Bhojpuri folk-songs* were published in 1887.* As editor and translator of folk-songs, Grierson found followers in A. G. SHIREFF,* Sarat Chandra MITRA* and Dinesh Chandra SEN.* From 1944 onwards a new impetus was given by VERRIER-ELWIN,* followed by S. C. DUBEY* and W. G. ARCHER.*

All those early works were published in English: they included English translations from the vernaculars, but usually did not give the text. For the last thirty years or so, those pioneers have been relieved by a new generation of Indian scholars, who set about collecting folk-songs composed all over Northern India in various Indo-Aryan dialects. Their books were mostly published in Hindi, and included the songs in the original dialect,

1. *Bārahmāsā*, Les Chansons des douze mois dans les litteratures indo-aryannes, par Charlotte Vaudeville, Institute Français Indologie, Pondichéry, 1965.

*Cf. Bibliography.

with a Hindi paraphrase. Collections of folk-songs were published *inter alia* by Devilal Sharma for Rajasthani, Induprakash Pande for Avadhi, Tej Narayan Lal for Maithili, Shyam Parmar for Malavi. The most prominent and most prolific among the new wave of Indian folklorists was Krishnadev Upadhyay, a scholar from Ballia in the heart of the Bhojpuri area, who took up the task of revealing the treasure of the Bhojpuri folk-songs: he collected about a thousand of them and published them in two volumes, with a Hindi translation.* The same scholar was also the author of other works dealing with the tradition of folk-songs and folk literature especially a study on "The background of Folk Literature"*, which included a precious bibliography listing the folk-songs edited in fifteen languages and dialects of Northern India up to 1957.

All the collections of folk-songs composed in the various languages and dialects of Northern India include a comparatively large number of so-called *BĀRAHMĀSĀ*, "Songs of the Twelve Months". Nearly all of them belong to the "Viraha-Bārahmāsā" type, on the theme of the pain of separation (*viraha*) endured by a young wife pining for the return of her beloved all through the twelve months of the year. In such songs, the description of nature is intimately and attractively joined to the expression of the heroine's sorrow. Such songs are essentially women's songs and must have been composed by village women. In their songs, the four months of the rainy season are given more importance than the other months of the year : the season of love and intimacy *par excellence* being also the most painful trial for the the loving wife separated from her mate.

So great are the charm and pathos of those songs and so powerful their appeal to Indian sensibility that the Bārahmāsā folk-song soon became a literary "genre": actually, a good many Bārahmāsās were composed by male poets—usually rural poets —and are being composed to this day. Most of those poems are *muktaka*, i.e. "independent" poems, with the male composer's name introduced in the last line in the traditional fashion, while the female poets remain for ever anonymous. But in all cases the Viraha Bārahmāsā is placed in the mouth of a "virahiṇī", a woman tormented by the absence of her lord.

*Cf. Bibliography.

A number of verses borrowed from village Bārahmāsās are found included in the ancient Rajasthani ballad known as *Ḍholā-mārū-rā dūhā* : in that famous legend, which has inspired so many miniature paintings in Rajasthan, both the heroines in turn appear as pathetic "virahiṇīs", pining for their common husband, Ḍholā. Other Bārahmāsās, mostly of the "didactic" type, are found inserted in the folk epics (also known as "folk-mahākāvyas") composed in medieval times by Hindu as well as Muslim poets. This is specially the case with the *mangal* literature of Medieval Bengal. Muslim poets were no less fond of the Bārahmāsā genre as were Hindu poets, as exemplified by the Sufi literature known as "Hindi *mathnavīs*" composed in the Avadhi dialect of eastern Hindi, from the 14th century onwards. The most ancient of these *mathnavīs*, the *Candāyan* of Mullā Dāūd, is based on an ancient Bhojpuri folk Epic known as "Lor-Candā", which depicts the adventures of the Ahīr hero Lor or Lorik, claimed by the ardent love of two touching "virahiṇīs", Mainā and Candā, as Ḍholā, the hero of the Rājasthānī Epic, is claimed by Mālvāṇī and Mārvūṇī. Contrary to the authors of the *mangal-kāvyas* in Bengali, the Sufi authors in Avadhi had no use for didactic Bārahmāsās : they invariably stuck to the "Viraha-Bārahmāsā", sung by a lovelorn heroine: for medieval Sufi poets, as later for the poets of Krishnaite bhakti, "love in separation" (*viraha-prema*)—which they took as an equivalent of the Arabic word '*ishq*'—was the most perfect form of love, especially divine love, as it expressed the torments experienced by the created soul in its search for the divine Beloved.

The fact that the Bārahmāsā genre was also used as a means of religious propaganda, first by Jaina monks and later by the "Sant" poets and the Sikh Gurus, could not but enhance its enduring prestige : the Bārahmāsā literature appears as the golden thread around which the souls of India's villagers, from remote ages to this day, have woven the web of their joys and sorrows, especially the sorrows of women's hearts—since the Viraha-Bārahmāsā remains originally and essentially the most perfect lyrical expression of the village women of northern India.

CONTENTS

*Unless indicated otherwise, all the translations are by the author. The originals in the Bengali and Gujarati scripts have been transliterated in the Nagari script.

A NOTE ON TRANSLITERATION

In Part I of this book, the internationally accepted mode of transliteration from the Sanskrit (Nāgarī) alphabet into the Roman character has been maintained throughout.

In Part II, which includes English translations from various Indo-Aryan vernaculars and notes, the transliteration has been simplified in order to make the text more easily readable to the non-Indologist:

(1) The Sanskrit final short *a*, no longer pronounced in the vernaculars, except after a double consonant, is not written; Sanskrit *kārttika* is written : *kārttik*.

(2) The Sanskrit vowel ṛ has been written *ri*, according to modern pronunciation : *kṛṣṇa* is written *krishna*.

(3) The two Sanskrit palatals, non-aspirate *c* and aspirate *ch* have been written *ch* and *chh* respectively : *caumāsā* is written *chaumāsā*, *chaymāsā*, *chhaymāsā*.

(4) The two Sanskrit sibilant *ś* and *ṣ*, no longer differentiated in pronunciation in the Indo-Aryan vernaculars, are both written *sh* : *pauṣa* is written *paush*; *āśvina*, *āshvin*.

(5) The distinction between the non-retroflex and the retroflex consonant, the latter marked by a dot underneath, has not been kept : *āṣāḍha* is written *āshādh*, *viṣṇu*, *vishnu*; *phālguna*, *phālgun*

PART I

BĀRAHMĀSĀ LITERATURE IN INDO-ARYAN VERNACULARS

1. ORIGIN AND DEVELOPMENT OF THE BĀRAHMĀSĀ FORM

The poetic form known as *bārahmāsā*, "twelve months", appeared at an early date in the vernacular literatures of Northern India. Its special characteristic is that it follows the twelve months of the year, one stanza being devoted to each. The genre was and still seems to be extraordinarily popular in the rural communities of Northern India, from Gujarat to Bengal. Lists of village songs in vernaculars published over the last twenty years contain a fairly large number of *bārahmāsā*s. In spite of being a very old form, the *bārahmāsā* still has an honoured place in tradition and is still being composed.

In addition to "twelve-months" songs, there are those listing only some of the months of the year (four, six or eight). These may be considered as "scaled-down models" of the main type. By far the most widespread is the *caumāsā* (*caumāsī*, *comāsī*), which lists the "four months" (Skt. *caturmāsya*) of the rainy season, from the month of Āṣāḍha to the month of Āśvina, occasionally from the month of Śrāvaṇa to the month of Kārttika.

This type of composition has only recently attracted the attention of critics and historians. A few *bārahmāsā*s were published or translated in various compilations at the end of the 19th century. In an article published in 1884, *Some Bihari Folk-Songs*,[1] G. Grierson gave a brief analysis of eighteen village songs collected in the Ara district in the heart of Bihar; the first seven belong to the *bārahmāsā* type, which Grierson calls a literary genre "well known in India since ancient times".

But the first translation of a *bārahmāsā* in a European language is probably the ballad entitled *The Koonbee's Grief*, in Forbes's *Rāsmālā*, published in 1856. This song lists the labours

1. JRAS, 1884, pp. 196 ff.

of a poor peasant (the *Kunbī*, burdened with taxes) in the form of a prayer to Kṛṣṇa.

Two articles by the Bikaner scholar Agarchand Nahta provide the groundwork for a study of the subject. In a first article, published in 1954[2], Nahta analyzes twenty or so *bārahmāsā*s from several manuscripts discovered in Bikaner. The first ten are *viraha-bārahmāsā*s concerned with Rājimatī's *viraha* for Neminātha; the last one is not a *bārahmāsā*, but a *ṣaḍ-ṛtu-varṇana*, a description of the six seasons of the year. An important article by the same author appeared in 1957, on "The ancient tradition of *bārahmāsā*s".[3] Nahta declares that his own collection of manuscripts (which is famous) includes over a hundred *bārahmāsā*s composed by Jain writers. Three-quarters are concerned with the famous Neminātha (the 22nd Jain *tīrthaṁkara*) and his wife, Rājimatī; two refer to Ṛṣabha, one to Pārśvanātha, five to Sthūlibhadra and two to other Jain *ācārya*s. Some of these poems, according to Nahta, are "ordinary *bārahmāsā*s" (i.e. enumerative ?). At the end of the article, the author gives the text of the *Bārah navaü* of Dharam Sūri, which he considers to be "the oldest known *bārahmāsā*".

A work in Bengali by Shivaprasad Bhattacharya appeared a little later on the other side of India, under the title "Indian Bārahmāsā Literature".[4] Notwithstanding the title, Bhattacharya confines his attention to Bengali writings. He raises the question of the *ādibārahmāsā* or the origin of *bārahmāsā*s, without greatly clarifying the matter, as the basic elements are not properly defined.

In an important article published in 1961, D. Zbavitel of the Prague Oriental Institute took up the question and tried to trace the development of *bāromāsī* literature (the Bengali form of *bārahmāsā*) in the province of Bengal. Although deliberately

2. Agarchand Nahta, *Rājasthān meṁ hindī ke hasta likhita granthoṁ kī khoj*, Vol. IV, Udaipur, 1884; Chap. 2: *Bārah māsā*, pp. 161 ff.

The first ten *bārahmāsā*s are *viraha-bārahmāsā*s, dealing with Rājimatī's *viraha* for Neminātha.

3. Agarchand Nahta, *Bārahmāsā kī pracīna paraṁparā*, "Hindi Anuśīlan", varṣa 6, V.S. 2010.

4. Shivaprasad Bhattacharya, *Bharatīya sahitye bāromāsya*, Calcutta, 1960.

restricted to Bengali *bāromāsī*s, "The development of the Baromasi in the Bengali literature"[5] is particularly significant in that it sets out the problem of the genre's origins and development, and also attempts to classify *bāromāsī*s into different types. I shall therefore be referring mainly to the work of A. Nahta and D. Zbavitel.[6]

2. THE OLDEST *BĀRAHMĀSĀ*S

The *bārahmasā* is a genre which belongs to the vernacular literature of India. There are no known examples of *bārahmāsā*s in Sanskrit,[7] only *ṣaḍ-ṛtu-varṇana*s, although certain early types of *dūta-kāvya* suggest that songs of the kind were known.[8]

The great majority of *bārahmāsā*s, simple village songs, obviously remain unpublished, being part of the great floating folk-song mass. A large number of specimens collected in various recent compilations of village songs are naturally modern in language and form. D. Zbavitel has made a first attempt at break-down by separating out the Bengali *baromāsī*s; the same should now be done for other Indo-Aryan languages and dialects.[9]

5. D. Zbavitel, *The development of the Baromasi in the Bengali Literature*, Archiv Orientalni 29, 1961, pp. 583 ff.

6. Information on recent *bārahmāsā*s composed by Sant or Sūfī poets can be found in D. P. Sinha, *Bhojpurī loka-gita meṁ karuṇa rasa*, Hindi Sahitya Sammelan, Allahabad, V.S. 2001; also in Parashuram Chaturvedi, *Santa kāvya*, 2nd edition, Kitab Mahal Allahabad, 1961, pp. 36-37.

7. The *Haṁsa-sandeśa*, which is said to have been composed in Sanskrit by Raghunāthdās, one of the "six Goswāmīs", successors to Caitanya (in the first half of the 16th century), has not been preserved; it is only known to us through the Bengali translation by Narasiṁhadās (17th century). The subject of the *Haṁsa-sandeśa* is the same as that of the work of the same name composed by another Vaishnava Goswāmī, Rūpa: the *gopī* Lalitā sends a *haṁsa*-bird to Kṛṣṇa with a message describing the sufferings of Rādhā and the *gopīs* separated from Him during the twelve months of the year. This is therefore a *viraha-bārahmāsā*, in the form of a *sandeśa*; cf. J. B. Chaudhuri. *The Haṁsa-dūta of Vāmana Bhaṭṭa Bāṇa*, Calcutta, 1941, pp. 39-40.

8. Cf. Ch. Vaudeville, *A Note on the Ghaṭakarpara and the Meghadūta*, Journal of the Oriental Institute of Baroda, Vol IX, No. 2, Dec. 1959, pp. 129-134.

9. C. Champion's recent thesis, entitled "Chants Populaires Bhojpuri, Matériaux pour l'étude de la littérature orale de l'Inde du Nord", defended

Besides these folk-songs, presumed to be modern, there is an important group of older *bārahmāsās*, either preserved as such or included in narrative works. These are mainly composed in three languages: Old Mārvāṛī-Gujarātī, also known as *māru-gurjāra*, which Tessitori calls "Old Western Rājasthānī" (OWR) and the Jain writers "Old Gujarātī" (OG), and which certain Indian writers consider to be a late form of "vulgar Apabhraṃśa"[10]; Old Bangālī and Classical Avadhī, the latter being a literary dialect based on the Eastern Hindi dialect spoken in the province of Oudh (Ayodhya). There is one *bārahmāsā* in Old Gujarātī attributed to the famous 15th century Vaishnava poet Narsī Mehtā : a *viraha-bārahmāsā* put into Rādhā's mouth.[11] The only specimen that could be found in Marāṭhī was composed at Tanjore (Tamil Nad) at the end of the 17th century.[12]

This essay is concerned with the oldest texts, which belong to folk literature. For from the 17th century onwards, this type of composition seems to have lost its appeal, at any rate as a lyrical form. The genre nevertheless survives into the 19th century, mainly as a didactic vehicle, with the "Sant" poets of the Kabīr tradition, and the Sīkh poets.[13]

The earliest Indo-Aryan vernacular period is still dimly lit. Few texts have yet been published and few of those are critically edited. Those which do exist are difficult for the uninitiated to appreciate. For this reason, Part II of this book consists of the

---

at the Université de Paris III in June 1983, though not yet published, is an important contribution to this field of study. Some 950 songs in Bhojpuri (published in K. D. Upadhyay's collection, Allahabad, Vol. I, 1954, Vol. II, 1956) are translated into French, with Introduction and notes. Some twenty of those songs are *bārahmāsās*.

10. Namvar Singh, in *Hindī ke vikās meṁ apabhraṁśa kā yog*, Allahabad, 9th edition, 1954, pp. 213 ff., gives the *Neminātha-caupāī* (*catuṣpadikā*) as "the oldest known Bārahmāsā" in "popular Apabhraṁśa" (*grāmya apabhraṁśa*); cf. Part II, Specimen VII.

11. The date traditionally attributed to Narsī Mehtā is 1414-1480. The *bārahmāsā* in question is included in I. S. Desai's large collection, *Bṛhat-kāvya-dohan*, Bombay, 1911, Vol. 7, pp. 27-29. It seems of doubtful authenticity.

12. This *bārahmāsā* is anonymous. One edition was found at Tanjore by Professor S. G. Tulpule; cf. Part II, Specimen VI.

13. Cf. pp. 42-44.

texts and annotated translations of a certain number of *bārahmāsā*s composed in languages of more or less archaic periods. Along with pure *bārahmāsā*s, we include two specimens of *caumāsā*s, "four months" (the rainy season): Rādhā's *comāsī*, from the *Śrikṛṣṇakīrtana* of Baḍu Caṇḍidās (15th/16th century)[14] and the *Thūlibhadda-phāgu* of Jinapadma Sūri, a Jain writer (c. 1330)[15] the latter being in effect a *caumāsā*. These two specimens throw valuable light on the development of *bārahmāsā* literature.

3. DIFFERENT TYPES OF *BĀRAHMĀSĀ*S

The classification of *bārahmāsā*s is a difficult matter, in view of the variety of forms encountered. Most *bārahmāsā*s are roughly divided into two types: *bārahmāsā*s of purely oral village tradition and literary *bārahmāsā*s, i.e. those belonging to written literature, the composition of which shows evidence of poetic or artistic care. Zbavitel has shown convincingly that the first type preceded the second and not vice-versa; in other words the "village" *bārahmāsā* is not a by-product or a rough imitation of an older, more refined literary type, in Sanskrit, Prākrit or Literary Apabhraṁśa. There is no reason to suppose that the *bārahmāsā* is derived from the *ṣaḍ-ṛtu-varṇana*, which seems to belong to *kāvya* literature; rather is it a parallel genre, rooted in peasant life : the cycle of agricultural labours and the succession of seasonal festivals over the twelve months of the solar year.

While the succession of the months is an essential element of the genre, the number of months considered is not. The songs known as *caumāsā*, *chaymāsā* and *aṣṭamāsā* are undeniably of the same type. It should be added, however, that only the *caumāsā* is found over a wide area and at an early date; *chaymāsā*s and *aṣṭamāsā*s are fairly rare and seem to be deviations of *bārahmāsā*s.[16] There is also the point that the *caumāsā* invari-

14. J. C. Ghosh, *Bengali Literature*, Oxford, 1948, p. 38, suggests that the *Śrīkṛṣṇakīrtana* should be dated to the 14th/15th century A.D.; Sukumar Sen, *History of Bengali Literature*, Sahitya Akademi, 1960, p. 71, considers that the language of the *Srīkṛṣṇakīrtana* places it in the 14th century rather than the 15th and that it may even be older.

15. Cf. Part II, Specimen VIII.

16. Cf. Zbavitel, op. cit., p. 512, note 2. The author considers that the number of the months listed is not a decisive factor in type classification.

ably describes the rainy season, never any other. Another important characteristic, to which we shall return, is that while the theme of *bārahmāsās* varies, the theme of the *caumāsā* is always the same : the *viraha* of a wife separated from her husband during the rainy season.

Zbavitel[17] proposes the classification of *bārahmāsās* (*bāromāsīs*) into five types :

(*a*) The religious *bārahmāsā*,

(*b*) The farmer's *bārahmāsā*,

(*c*) The narrative *bārahmāsā* (included in an "epic" poem),

(*d*) The *viraha-bārahmāsā*, concerned with the sufferings of a wife separated from her husband during the twelve months of the year,

(*e*) The "trial of chastity" *bārahmāsā*.

Zbavitel considers types (*a*) and (*b*) as the oldest. Indeed it seems probable that the poetic form of the *bārahmāsā*, in its early simplicity, was first used for mnemonic or other practical purposes. The example of a "religious *bārahmāsā*" given by Zbavitel is nothing more than a sort of catalogue of the main festivals celebrated in Bengali villages throughout the year. The specimen quoted as an example of a "farmer's *bārahmāsā*" lists the main agricultural labours over the twelve-month cycle. The author considers types (*a*) and (*b*) as "relics of a type which must have flourished in a distant past" and presumes that these two types disappeared or fell into disuse when other more elaborate types appeared.

However, the distinction between "religious" and "farmer's" *bārahmāsās* does not seem entirely justified, since it is based on the purpose of the type rather than its inherent characteristics. In reality they make up one single type : the enumerative or mnemotechnic *bārahmāsā*. The *Ḍāker vacana* in old Bengali (see Part II, Specimen I) also comes under this heading. Whether the poem lists festivals during the year or labours in the fields,

---

It should, however, be noted that the *chaymāsā* ("six months") which seems to be fairly widespread in the east (in Mithilā and Bengal) is rarely found in the west. As for the *caumāsā*, inasmuch as it precedes the *bārahmāsā* of separation and explains it, it poses a separate problem; see pp. 27-30.

17. Zbavitel, op. cit., pp. 585 ff.: *Basic types of folk-Baromasi*.

it remains a kind of peasant calendar.[18] It is a simple framework making it possible to memorize a series of events occurring in a given order, which is determined either by nature or custom, the latter, to a peasant mind, being as immutable as the former. This kind of composition is still extremely popular in rural areas, as is shown by the number of examples in recent compilations of village songs. Thus D. P. Sinha, in his collection of songs in the Bhojpuri dialect, gives a *bārahmāsā* concerned with the conception and birth of a child, viewed by a mother; the poem begins with the wedding in the month of Jeṭh (most favoured month for weddings) and ends in the month of Baisākh with the religious ceremony of *chaṭha vrata* performed by the mother in the month after the birth.[19] *Bārahmāsā*s dealing with the different aspects of peasant life are noticeably didactic in style; the descriptive element is reduced to nothing or nearly so, and the lyrical expression of feelings is excluded. But if Euclid can be put into sonnets, the more easily can a *bārahmāsā* be used to describe village customs. This type is certainly very old and has stayed in continuous use.

The third type of *bārahmāsā* identified by Zbavitel, the "narrative *barahmasa*", is one which is "an integral part of a longer epic work". The term "narrative", however, is slightly confusing; the fact that a *bārahmāsā* is included in a narrative work does not imply that the *bārahmāsā* itself is narrative in character. Zbavitel emphasizes the flexibility of the genre and in fact notes that "epic or narrative Baromasis" included in the Bengali *maṅgal-kāvya* never constitute an integral part of the work in which they occur :

18. Compare the specimens of the two types: (1) Religious baromāsī and (2) Farmer's baromāsī, given by Zbavitel, op. cit., pp. 586-587:

(1) In Paush, there is the festival of guardians, cakes in every house.
In Māgh, there is Śrīpanchamī, chalk in the boy's hand.
In Phālgun, there is the Dol festival, red powder is scattered.

(2) In Paush, I brought offerings to the feet of the house-God.
In Māgh, I touched the feet of the Goddess Earth.
In Phālgun, I took the plough, in Chaitra the seed.

These two *bāromāsī*s seem to belong to the same type, namely the mnemotechnic or didactic type.

19. D. P. Sinha, op. cit., p. 325.

"The Baromasi never developed, in any *mangal-kāvya* or other epic composition, into a compulsory part of it. It always depended purely on the author's decision whether to enrich his poem by a Baromasi or not. The Baromasi seems to have made its way into the epic poetry of classical Bengali literature from outside, from the folk-poetry; and its use by a poet in this or that composition may, besides other factors, conceal a hint of his relation to folk-poetry and his intention to be as popular as possible, not to be heard only by Rajas and their courtiers but by the village folks whose favorite the Baromasi was."[20]

*Baromāsī*s (and also *chaymāsī*s and *aṣṭamāsī*s) which occur in the Bengali *maṅgal-kāvya* are mainly of the didactic type. The theme varies considerably, as the *bārahmāsā* provides poets with a popular form perfectly adaptable to all types of teaching or scholarly digression. For example, in Vipradās's *Manasā-maṅgala*, the goddess Manasā explains to the gods how she has been offended by the merchand Chand over a whole year, and her speech is in the *baromāsī* form. Similarly, the two versions of the *Caṇḍī-maṅgala* composed by the poets Dvija Madhab and Mukundram Chakravarti each include three *bāromāsī*s spoken by the three heroines, Phullarā, Khullanā and Suśīlā. Khullanā's *baromāsī* describes the pain of separation from her husband, but in spite of the theme this *bāromāsī* is not a *viraha-bārahmāsā* : the heroine's physical sufferings are simply listed,with no lyrical or sentimental element.[21]

In Bengal, at least up to fairly recent times, narrative works do not contain *viraha-bārahmāsā*s; this type is found exclusively

20. Zbavitel, op. cit., p. 608.

21. The anomaly of this fact has been rightly pointed out by Zbavitel: "It is really surprising, especially in the case of Khullanā's Baromasi, in *Chaṇḍī-mangal*, where the situation is literally a challenge to insert a Baromasi proper, speaking of the longings of the heroine for her absent husband; but its theme is, for the most part, her physical troubles during the twelve months of separation" (op. cit., p. 609).

In other words, instead of the expected *viraha-bārahmāsā*, we find a didactic *bārahmāsā*.

As regards these legends and Bengali *maṅgala* literature, cf. D. C. Sen, *History of the Bengali Language and Literature*, 2nd edition, University of Calcutta, 1954, pp. 267-299; also D. Zbavitel, *Bengali Folk-Ballads of Mymensingh*. University of Calcutta, 1963.

as independent poems, known as *biraha-kahinī*s, in numerous collections of vishnuite *pada*s on the theme of the loves of Rādhā and Kṛṣṇa, which has led Zbavitel to suggest that the evolution of the didactic *bārahmāsā* into a *viraha-bārahmāsā* could have been due to vishnuite influence. However, it is interesting to note that among Bengali *biraha-kahinī*s the *chaumāsā* (*chomāsī*) type appears earlier than the *bārahmāsā* (*bāromāsī*) type. The *Śrīkṛṣṇakīrtana* of Baḍu Caṇḍīdās, which probably dates from the 15th century, includes a *caumāsā* in the last part of the poem entitled *Rādhāviraha*[22] We shall be returning to the connection between the *caumāsā* and the *bārahmāsā*.

In contrast to Bengali literature, Western literatures in Old Gujarātī (OG) and Avadhī include *viraha-bārahmāsā*s in narrative works, usually verse novels, from the 14th century onwards. The oldest specimen of a *bārahmāsā* included in a narrative work seems to be Mainā's *bārahmāsā*, found in the *Candāyan*, the first *mathnavī* in Avadhī, composed by the Muslim poet Mullā Dāūd in 1375.[23] The *Candāyan* is a Sūfī version of the famous legend of Lorik and Candā. Abandoned by her husband "Lor" or "Lorik", who has left to search for the beautiful Candā, Lorik's wife, Mainā, gives vent to her pain in a "message" (*sandeśa*), which takes the form of a *viraha-bārahmāsā*.[24]

22. See above, note 14 and pp. 27-30; translated in Part II, Specimen II.

23. The material available is not sufficient to indicate the existence of a legend of Mainā apart from the legend of Lorik and Candā. But the popularity of this legend is likely to have inspired *caumāsā*s and *viraha-bārāhmāsā*s put into the mouth of the *satī* Mainā; Mainā's *bārahmāsā* sometimes occurs in isolation from the legend in which it is inserted. In any case it is probable that Mainā's *bārahmāsā* was already part of the oral tradition of the legend of Lorik and Candā, written down by Mullā Dāūd in the 14th century.

24. There are two editions of Mullā Dāūd's *Candāyan*:

(1) edited by P. L. Gupta, Bombay, 1964; (2) edited by M. P. Gupta, Agra, 1967. In both editions, Mainā's *viraha-gīta* begins with the month of Sāvan (*śrāvaṇa*), but in the P. L. Gupta edition this song covers only eight months, from Sāvan to Phālgun; it is therefore an *aṣṭamāsā*; in the M. P. Gupta edition it includes all the twelve months (stanzas 343-354).

In Avadhī verse novels, the *viraha-bārahmāsā* is not an integral part of the story but simply an ornament, a sort of lyrical variation on the theme of the *viraha* of a faithful wife. The *viraha-bārahmāsā* is never put into the mouth of the main heroine, but given to her rival, the first, neglected wife: Mainā in Mullā Dāūd's *Candāyan*, Rūpman in Sheikh Qutban's *Mṛgavatī*, Nāgamatī in Muhammad Jāyasī's *Padmāvat*. The piece is often highly lyrical, but could easily be omitted without affecting the development of the story. This is in contrast with Rājasthānī literature, where the *bārahmāsā* usually forms the nucleus of the work in which it is inserted: a simple ballad woven around the theme of separation of husband and wife. A typical example of this kind of composition can be found in the *Bīsaldev-rās*, attributed to the poet Nalha Kavi[25], and in the *Mainäsat* attributed to the poet "Sādhan"[26].

Even in this case, the narrative element in the *bārahmāsā* itself is practically negligeable. For example an analysis of the *Bīsaldev-rās*, (in the Gupta and Nahta edition), shows that the events described in the rest of the legend have been somewhat artificially adjusted to accommodate the *bārahmāsā*, with the result that there are odd variations in tone and vocabulary between the *bārahmāsā* text and the text of the narrative in which it occurs. The purely narrative part is always in juxta-

25. There are two editions of the *Bīsaldev-rās:* (1) *Bīsaldev rāso*, edited by Satyajivan Varma, N.P.S., Banaras, V. S. 1982; (2) *Bīsal dev rās*, edited by M. P. Gupta and A Nahta, 1st edition, Allahabad, 1953.

26. *Sādhan-kṛt mainā-sat*, edited by H. H. N. Dvivedi, Gwalior, 1959. The attribution of the Mainā-sat to the poet "Sādhan", accepted by A. Nahta, M. P. Gupta and H. H. N. Dvivedi, is doubtful. It seems that this attribution is based on incorrect word division: *sādhana* instead of *sā dhana*, meaning the wife (*dhana*) both in Mainā's *bārahmāsā* and Rājimatī's *bārahmāsā*, found in the version of the *Bīsaldev-rās* published by A. Nahta and M. P. Gupta. This *Bīsaldev-rās*, of which no old manuscript is extant (the oldest being dated S. 1633), seems to be a *reficiamento* of an old *Rājimatī-sāt*, the trial of chastity of Rājimatī, of a type similar to the *Mainā-sat*. Indeed the whole of tradition associates Rājimatī's *viraha* with the renunciation of the world by her fiancé, the Jain *tīrthaṁkara*, Nemi-nātha. Rājimatī's *bārahmāsā*, which is common to all manuscripts, appears as the nucleus of the *Bīsaldev-rās*; the relation of Rājimatī to Bīsaldev is somewhat uncertain.

position to the *viraha-bārahmāsā*. The latter forming a separate type, will be studied later.

The type which Zbavitel calls "Baromasi of Test" is concerned with a trial, generally a temptation, imposed on a young wife separated from her husband. However, the conditions and circumstances in which this trial takes place are not mentioned in the *bārahmāsā* itself, but only in an introductory narrative passage. The temptation itself takes the form of a dialogue between the *virahiṇī* and a *dutī* or *kuṭanī* (go-between), or again between the *virahiṇī* and her companion (*sakhī*) who invites her to forget the faithless spouse and enjoy her fleeting youth.

The trial of chastity imposed on the *virahiṇī* sometimes occurs before the *viraha-bārahmāsā*, but more usually immediately after, as is the case in the *Bīsaldev-rās* in the *Maināsat* already mentioned.

Occasionally the temptation is inserted in the *bārahmāsā* itself; this is the case in one of the oldest *bārahmāsā*s which have come down to us, Vinayacandra Sūri's *Nemināṭha-catuṣpadikā* in Old Gujarātī[27] (see Part II, Specimen VII). In this poem the description of each month begins with a verse *a* from the wife bemoaning the absence of the husband; followed by a short dialogue in two verses, *b* and *c* : verse *b* from a *sakhī*, who urges the heroine to enjoy her youth without waiting for the husband's problematical return; verse *c* from the young woman, rejecting the temptation and declaring her unshakeable fidelity to the absent spouse. However, even here, where lamentation and temptation are interwoven, it is clear that the dialogue which occurs in verses *b and c* of each month is independent from the lamentation expressed in verse *a*; there is no continuity between verses *a* and *b*. The dialogue, i.e. the whole sequence of verses *b* and *c*, could quite easily be shifted to follow the sequence of the *a* verses, which constitute a *viraha-bārahmāsā*. These are two quite different forms of composition, linked by an association of ideas: inasmuch

27. 1st edition in *Pracīna Gurjara Kāvya Sangraha*, G.O.S. XIII, by C. D. Dalal; 2nd edition in *Jaina Gurjara Kāvya*, 1926, by Mohanlal Dalicand; 3rd edition in *Jaina Śvetāmbara Conference Herald*, by Jinavijaya Muni; 4th edition in *Śrī Forbes Gujarātī Sabhā Granthāvalī*, Bombay, 1955, by H. C. Bhayani. According to this last author, the work may be dated to the early part of the 14th century.

as the heroine is suffering, she must also be tempted, her victory over temptation adding to her dazzling merits and the pathos of the situation. It is for this reason that we often find the lyrical effusions of the *viraha-bārahmāsā* associated with an attempt at seduction which is invariable repulsed by the *virahiṇī*, who is also a *satī*.[28]

Here again the Bengali tradition seems to diverge from the older Western tradition. In a certain number of *bāromāsī*s found in East Bengal, it is the husband who deceitfully plays the part of the seducer and puts his young wife's chastity to the test over twelve consecutive months. But, as Zbavitel suggests, this type must be comparatively recent, for there is no trace of it in classical literature. The same author mentions another type of "Baromasi of Test", where the seducer is not the husband, but a third person addressing the young wife: in each month there is a new attempt, followed by a new failure; in the twelfth month the husband returns. This type, which shows no signs of antiquity, is not a *viraha-bārahmāsā*; the lyrical and descriptive element is missing, although the third person sometimes describes the supposed sufferings of the seducer in order to apply pressure on the young wife, always without success.

It now remains to study the *viraha-bārahmāsā*, both its basic characteristics and its evolution.

4. THE *VIRAHA-BĀRAHMĀSĀ*, A FOLK-LYRIC

The great majority of *bārahmāsā*s found in written Indo-Aryan literatures are *viraha-bārahmāsā*s or "*bārahmāsā*s of separation". Almost all *bārahmāsā*s prior to 1600, with the exception of Manasā's *bārahmāsā* in Vipradās's *Manasā-maṅgal* in Bengali, mentioned above (see p. 10) belong to this type; they are lyrical songs or pieces put into the mouth of a wife or neglected mistress, bemoaning her sufferings during the twelve months of separation.

We have seen that most romanesque works in Old Gujarātī and Avadhī, before 1600, included *bārahmāsā*s of this kind. The type also occurs frequently in Bengali literature (though less

28. Cf. Nahta, *Sat saṁjñaka racnāoṁ kī paraṁparā*, Rashtrabharati, May, 1956.

early)[29], in the form of *biraha-kahinīs*, short independent lyrics or *padas* put almost invariable into the mouth of Rādhā languishing during the absence of Kṛṣṇa. All collections of vishnuite *padas* on the Kṛṣṇa-Rādhā theme contain a fairly large number of them.

Whether an independent poem or part of a narrative work, the *viraha-bārahmāsā* (type *d* in Zbavitel's classification) is essentially a lyrical form : a complaint sung by a young woman separated from the one she loves. The presentation of the characters and the account of the circumstances which led to their separation are almost always passed over in silence, or mentioned briefly in the stanza or half-stanza which introduces the twelve stanzas, or groups of the twelve months. The conclusion is dealt with equally summarily. If the husband does not return, there is no conclusion; if he returns, his return is briefly indicated in one single line. Zbavitel notes that in Bengali *bārahmāsās* this is often a stereotyped sentence, such as :

"Here comes my dear husband, a canopy over his head !"

In Vinayacandra Sūri's *Nemināṭha-catuṣpadikā*, mentioned earlier, it is a sort of refrain (perhaps simply a popular saying) which serves both as introduction and conclusion to the *bārahmāsā* of Rājimatī or Rājal :

"For the love of Nemi, on Girnār,
Princess Rājal became a Siddhī !"

In the *viraha-bārahmāsā*, the list of the twelve months is not merely a framework for one content or another. There is always

29. Although modern in language and presentation, various *bārahmāsās* on the theme of Rādhā's *viraha* for Kṛṣṇa in Bengal and Bihar, are often attributed to Vidyāpati (cf. D. P. Sinha, op. cit., pp. 325 ff.). However, the poet Vidyāpati, born towards the end of the 14th century (hence a contemporary of Caṇḍīdās), is not really a Bengali poet, although his fame is as great in Bengal as in his own country, Mithilā, and Bengal has always claimed him as its own. Vidyāpati, the author of several works in Sanskrit, is known mainly for his lyrical poems in Maithilī dialect on the theme of the loves of Kṛṣṇa and Rādhā. In the songs known as *Mathurā*, Vidyāpati describes the *viraha* endured by Rādhā and the *gopīs* of the Vṛndāvana during Kṛṣṇa's absence. However, it does not seem that Vidyāpati ever adopted the folk form of the *caumāsā* or the *bārahmāsā*. Caṇḍīdās never composed *bārahmāsās*, but, as we have seen, a *caumāsā* is included in the *Rādhā-viraha* of the *Srīkṛṣṇakīrtana*.

a link between the heroine's feelings and the description of nature during the month in question. This combination of the descriptive element with the pathetic element in an inseparable whole is a basic feature of the *viraha-bārahmāsā*, the objects or phenomena described having a symbolic meaning or an affective resonance which is immediately comprehended by the peasant mind: the clouds of the month of Āṣāḍha, the night calls of water birds; others have a sexual connotation—the Holi game, the ripe mango whose juice runs in vain, the swing, and so on.

GENESIS OF THE *VIRAHA-BĀRAHMĀSĀ*

Would it be valid to suggest that the presumedly primitive type of the mnemotechnic or enumerative *bārahmāsā*, already analyzed, could have given birth to the *viraha-bārahmāsā* ? A first difficulty lies in the fact that no specimen of such early type of *bārahmāsā* has been found in any written literature prior to the appearance of the *viraha-bārahmāsā*.[30] And while it is easy to see how the enumerative type could have developed into the didactic type, the transition from the enumerative type to the lyrical *viraha-bārahmāsā*. would be hard to explain. There is no trace of a purely descriptive *bārahmāsā*, and no reason to suppose that pure description (if such there has ever been) would have become pathetic description or lyrical complaint under an outside influence.

D. Zbavitel wonders whether the krishnaite wave which invaded Bengal and Bihar in the 15th/16th centuries could have been the determining factor in the appearance of *viraha-bārahmāsās*. In Bengal, the *biraha-kahinī* is invariably linked with the legendary couple Rādhā-Kṛṣṇa, from the time of Caṇḍīdās and Vidyāpati :

"This type of Baromasi had been a favourite with the

30. The *Ḍaker vacana*, "Aphorisms of Ḍak" (lit. "The wiseacre's dicta"), an anonymous work in Old Bengali, is perhaps an exception, being a mnemotechnic *bārahmāsā* of an ancient type (cf. Part II, Specimen I). The language, however, seems relatively modern, as J. G. Ghosh points out (1948, p. 30). The date of composition of the *Ḍaker vacana* and the *Khanār vacana* remains uncertain.

Vaishnava poets since the 15th century; its theme is the separation of Rādhā from Kṛṣṇa and the description of her sorrows. It is possible that these Vaishnava poems, whose popularity among the widest classes of Bengali inhabitance is beyond any doubt, influenced folk-poetry to such extent that they actually gave impulse to the transformation of the descriptive Baromasi into these songs of separation. It must be admitted, however, that the reverse process is not inconceivable—that it was the folk-Baromasi of this type then already developed which forced an entry into Vaishnava poetry. The Vaishnavas were always eager enough to elicit a response among the people of Bengal, to use forms dear to the hearts of the country-folk. Another argument supporting this latter suggestion is the fact that, in the Rādhā-Kṛṣṇa legend, the separation was originally not described as lasting for a full year, so that the Baromasi does not seem to be fully in place here and looks more like a later insertion."[31]

But the popularity of the Kṛṣṇa legend does not explain how the *viraha-bārahmāsā* could have evolved from the "descriptive Baromasi", albeit that the appearance of the "Baromasi of separation" seems to coincide in Bengal with the development of Kṛṣṇa worship. Zbavitel notes in passing that the oldest *biraha-kahinī*s dealing with the Kṛṣṇa legend are not *bārahmāsā*s but *caumāsā*s ("four-month" songs). This suggests that the lyrical type of *viraha-bārahmāsā* must have sprung from a different root; and indeed it is difficult to see how the didactic *bārahmāsā* could have turned into a *viraha-bārahmāsā*. In addition, the oldest known *viraha-bārahmāsa*s are not krishnaite poems in Bengali but Jain works in Apabhraṁśa or old Mārvāṛī-Gujarātī; the heroes are not Kṛṣṇa and Rādhā, but one of the Jain saints, usually the romantic Nemi (Nemināthа) and his fiancée Rājimatī, cruelly abandoned by him on her wedding day.

In order to throw light on the origins of the *viraha-bārahmāsā* and its relationship to other forms of *bārahmāsā*s, it may be useful to analyze a fairly unusual example, the *Bārah navaü* or "Twelve Praises" of Dharam Sūri. The editor of this poem,

31. Zbavitel, op. cit., pp. 589-590.

A. Nahta, in the article already mentioned, considers it to be "the oldest known *bārahmāsā*".[32]

a. The *Bārah navaü*

This short poem of 13 stanzas, the author of which is unknown, was taken by A. Nahta from a manuscript discovered at Patan, which Nahta dates to the 12th/13th century V. S. (i.e. late 12th century A.D.). It consists of the panegyric of a certain Jain *muni* by the name of Dharam Sūri, in the form of a *bārahmāsā*. The text published by Nahta is based on one manuscript and unfortunately appears very corrupt: it is a mixture of prose and verse in late Apabhraṁśa, mixed with old Gujarātī forms, and the metre of the poetic sections is completely irregular. The first verse introduces Dharam Sūri:

"Hear the praise of Dharam Sūrī,
Jewel of the three worlds..."

The first and last stanzas describe the month of Sāvan (*śrāvaṇa*) and there is mention of *kuvalaya* and *mālatī* flowers, clouds, dancing peacocks and so on. From there we move on to Dharam Sūri, whose glory "is like the sun", then we pass to the month of Bhādon (*bhādra*). The whole poem is nothing but a series of jumps between the months of the year and the virtues of the said Dharam Sūri.

The first line of stanza 7 is a half-dohā (distich) which abruptly introduces a *virahiṇī*:

"The Gujjarī said: Come, my beloved, grant my desire!"

Next comes a song about peacocks, the heart of the *virahiṇī* (*virahiyā hṛdaya*) and a camel (*karaha*). The month of Phālgun is omitted, but the mention of the month of Caitra introduces another song, concerning the *mālatī* flower. Further on, there is a

32. A Nahta, V. S. 2010, pp. 39 ff. At the end of his article on "The ancient tradition of Bārahmāsās", the author gives the text of the *Bārah navaü* (pp. 45-46), as contained in a ms discovered at Patan in Gujarat. It should be noted, however, that this work is not called a *bārahmāsā* but a *bārah navaü*, "twelve praises", a title which corresponds to its didactic nature. Garcin de Tassy (H.L.H.H. Vol. II, p. 186, note 4) mentions a "Hindi" *barahmāsā* on the god Hara (Śiva), printed in Delhi in 1868 and entitled *Hara nāma kā bārahmāsā* : "Bārahmāsā in praise of Hara's name.

reproach from a *sahī* (*sakhī*): "Oh, my friend!". From stanza 12 onwards, there are refrains a few syllables long, interjections or onomatopeia, which are frequent in village songs. The month of Kārttika, for instance, introduces the song *pelli na*: "Do not leave !". There is every justification for doubting the authenticity of such a work, at least in the form given in the manuscript published by Nahta. Nevertheless, the specimen is interesting, since it is an attempt to combine a "religious" or didactic *bārahmāsā* with fragments of songs on the *viraha* theme (*viraha-gīta*).

These fragments have apparently been borrowed from two types well-known in Western India: rain songs, known as *caumāsā*s or *sāvan*s [*śrāvaṇa*], and songs of the month of Kārttika, i.e. autumnal songs known as *akṣepokti*s. The rain songs speak of the sorrow of a *virahiṇī* (once called a *gujjarī*) while the autumn songs are concerned with a wife's opposition to her husband's departure. The whole is completely incoherent: what link can there be between the succession of the twelve months, the great virtues of Dharam Sūri and the *viraha* of the *gujjarī* ? It seems that this *Bārah navaü* represents an old type of "religious" or didactic *bārahmāsā* composed by a Jain author to disseminate his teachings. But here and there, in the succession of the twelve months, fragments of folk-songs on the *viraha* theme have been incorporated. The incoherence of the text makes it impossible to consider this piece as a link between the didactic *bārahmāsā* and the *bārahmāsā* of separation : the dissimilar elements are not combined but juxtaposed. Yet the very juxtaposition sets a problem by suggesting that there has been interference between the didactic *bārahmāsā* and the folk-song on the *viraha* theme.

b. *Viraha-bārahmāsā* and *ṣad-ṛtu-varṇana*

Some authors tend to see in the *bārahmāsā* a type derived from the Sanskrit *ṣaḍ-ṛtu-varṇana* ("description of the six seasons"); some even include an occasional *ṣaḍ-ṛtu-varṇana* in a list of *bārahmāsā*s. In reality they are parallel but quite separate genres. The *ṣaḍ-ṛtu-varṇana*, as it appears in *kāvya* literature in Sanskrit, Prakrit and Apabhraṁśa, brilliantly describes the "six seasons" of the Indian year, with the suggestion of the pleasures of love being continually associated with the description of nature. The association of the erotic theme with the description of nature is a constant of the village song, as of the refined poetry of the *kāvya*, which does not mean that the village song itself borrowed this element from the *kāvya*. When compared with the *ṣaḍ-ṛtu-varṇana*, the *viraha-bārahmāsā* appears as an original type, quite different in form and content : a lyric type par excellence, a nostalgic song where description is fairly succinct—nature simply provides a background and a sort of echo to the pathetic longings of a young woman left alone.

Moreover, the combination of the description of nature and the *viraha* theme which characterizes the *viraha-bārahmāsā* is never found in the *ṣaḍ-ṛtu-varṇana*. One is tempted to attribute this to a simple difference in style and inspiration between Sanskrit literature and vernacular literatures. However, *mahākāvya* literature in Indo-Aryan vernaculars contains a fairly large number of *ṣaḍ-ṛtu-varṇana*s, the style of which is influenced by that of the Sanskrit *mahākāvya*s. And none of these poems combines the *viraha* theme with the description of the six seasons.[33] Muhammad Jāyasī's *Padmāvat*, which is both a *mathnavī* inspired by the Persian tradition and a sort of *mahākāvya* in Avadhī, even includes, one after the other, specimens of the two types of composition : a *viraha-bārahmāsā*, put into the mouth of Nāgamatī, the neglected wife of the hero, Ratansen, and a *ṣaḍ-ṛtu-varṇana*, which throughout its length describes the amorous pleasures of Ratansen and Padmāvatī during the six seasons of the year. A comparison of the two passages shows that Jāyasī deliberately borrowed from two different sources : the *viraha-bārahmāsā* from the village song tradition, the *ṣaḍ-ṛtu-varṇana* from the *mahākāvya* tradition. In the former the description of nature is associated with the lyrical expression of the wife's *viraha*; in the latter it accompanies a description of the lovers' pleasures, and becomes a kind of illustration of erotic treatises.

33. The *Sandeśa-rāsaka* of the Muslim poet Abdul Rahman in Apabhraṁśa contains a description of the pleasures of *saṁyoga* in the form of a *ṣad-ṛtu-varṇana*; so does the *Mādhavānala-Kāmakandalā* of Kuśallābh in OG.

c. *Viraha-barahmāsā*, *phāgu* and *rāsa*

Another type of folk literature which can usefully be compared with the *bārahmāsā* is the *phāgu* or *basant*, "spring song". *Phāgu* literature in Apabhraṁśa and OG is extremely ancient, comprising what are probably some of the oldest vernacular texts of Northern India. As K.M. Munshi[34] and K.B. Vyas[35] have shown, the *phāgu* is a variety of *rāsa* (*raso*, *rās*) : a sort of popular entertainment, mimed, sung and danced, similar to the *jātra* (*yātra*) of Bengal. The word *phāgu* (Skt. *phālguna*, Ap. *phaggu*, OG. *phāgu*, Hindi, Bengali *phāg*) refers to the spring game of Holī, in which people throw red powder or red water over each other (Skt. *phalgu*, "red").

The main and almost sole theme of the *phāgu* is the erotic theme in its various aspects and phases : *viyoga* and *saṁyoga*, union and separation of lovers. In his preface to the *Vasanta-vilāsa*, an ancient "profane" (i.e. non-Jain) *phāgu*, K.B. Vyas summarizes the main characteristics of the genre as follows :

> "A phagu usually commences with the description of spring —the splendour of the forest in spring, with the mango-trees blossoming, the Ketakī spreading its fragrance, the Aśoka richly laden with new foliage and the whole region resounding with the sweet notes of the cuckoo and the hum of bees.
>
> Then follows the description of the heroine separated from her husband and pining. The splendour of the season has no joy for her; her heart is sore for her loved one is away. Then the heroine is described as meeting with good omens like the throbbing of her limbs and the cawing of the crow in the morning which portend an early return of her husband. The husband returns from his long and arduous journey; the lover and the beloved are reunited. And now life puts on a new garb; everything takes on a new aspect. And here the author gets an opportunity, which he seizes and

34. K. M. Munshi, *Gujarāt and its Literature*, 2nd edition, Bombay, 1954.

35. K. B. Vyās, *Vasanta-vilāsa, an old Gujarātī Phāgu*, Bombay, 1942, Introd. pp. xxxvii ff.: *The Phāgu form, its characteristics*. The *Vasanta-vilāsa* has been critically edited and translated into English, with an introduction by W. Norman Brown, Newhaven, 1962.

turns to good account, of describing the personal charms of the heroine, the details of her toilet, ornaments and dress, ending it all with the description of the amorous sports of the reunited couple."[36]

The two protagonists of the *phāgu* belong to the Yādava tribe and the hero himself is sometimes called "the dark-complexioned Yādao". The latter is often Kṛṣṇa, the Yādava hero par excellence; however, in the oldest *phāgu*s which have come down to us, which are Jain works, the hero is invariably one of the Jain *tīrthaṁkara*s, for instance Sthūlibhadra, Pārśvanātha or Neminātha, usually Neminātha. The name of the young woman is not always given. She is often called simply *dhana* (the wife). When the hero is Kṛṣṇa, the young woman is his wife Rukmiṇī or Rādhā, the eternal *gopī* of the Vṛndāvana; when the hero is Sthūlibhadra, she is the courtesan Kośā; when the hero is Nemikumāra or Neminātha, she is Princess Rājal or Rājimatī, daughter of the Yādava King Ugrasena. The krishnaite form of the *phāgu* is not noticeably different from the Jain form : Kṛṣṇa takes the place of Nemi and, in the east (i.e. Bihar and Bengal) the *gopī* Rādhā takes the place of Rukmiṇī.[37]

The *phāgu* has certain traits in common with the *viraha-bārahmāsā*: both are folk forms, linked with village traditions; both associate the description of nature with the lyrical expression of amorous feeling. But in contrast to the *viraha-bārahmāsā* the *phāgu* is not a purely or mainly lyrical type; in the oldest *phāgu*s, at any rate, the "play-acting" element is always noticeable. The description of spring forms a changing framework, a succession of backgrounds for the two main characters, whose beauty and adornment are described at length. The songs, which are vehicles for the lyrical expression of feelings, alternate with an account of the actions of the two heroes. In the songs themselves, the *viraha* is given to the heroine, but this *viraha* is simply a phase in the development of the dramatic action : the necessary prelude to the joys of reunion and amorous pleasures. The dominant

36. K. B. Vyas, op. cit., p. xxxviii.

37. According to A. Nahta [V. S. 2010] a large number of *phāgu*s on the theme of Rājimatī and Neminātha are extant in Jain OG literature. In an article in Gujarātī, published in *Jaina Satya Prakāśa*, varṣa II, ank 6, pp. 169ff., H.R. Kapadia gives useful information on *phāgu* literature and a list of *phāgu*s published to date.

atmosphere is spring gaiety and joie de vivre. The nostalgic tone of the *viraha-bārahmāsā* is not much in evidence in the *phāgu.*

d. The Jain *phāgu* in Old Gujarātī

Though far-removed in spirit from the ascetic ideal of the Jains, the *phāgu* was nonetheless cultivated by them as a means of disseminating their teachings. In fact the oldest *phāgu*s which have come down to us are by Jain authors : the *Sirī-Thūlibhaddu* [*Śrī-Sthūlibhadra*] *phāgu* of Jinapadma Sūri (c. 1334) and the *Neminātha-phāgu* of Rājaśekhara Sūri (c. 1349).[38]

The *Neminātha-phāgu* is a fairly good illustration of the traditional features of the *phāgu,* in spite of its pathetic theme, borrowed from a famous Jain legend : the withdrawal from the world of the Yādava Prince Nemi (cousin to Kṛṣṇa) on the day he is to be married to Princess Rājimatī, daughter of Ugrasena, As the wedding procession arrives at Ugrasena's palace, Nemi sees in one of the palace courtyards the flock of animals that his future father-in-law is preparing to slaughter for the wedding feast. Moved with compassion, the young man decides to save their lives : he walks away, renouncing the ways of the world and his fiancée, Rājimatī, and retires to the holy mountain of Girnar. Later, he will be joined there by the unhappy Rājimatī, whose sufferings at being separated from Nemi have finally led to the same renunciation.

This legend is the foundation for innumerable *viraha-bārahmāsas* : the unfortunate Rājimatī laments for twelve months while waiting in vain for her Nemi, before embracing the ascetic

38. Ist edition of the *Neminātha-phāgu* of Rājaśekhara Sūri in *Pracīna kāvya-sangraha,* by O.D. Dalal, G.O.S.XIII: re-published in *Gurjararasāvali,* G.O.R. CXIII, Baroda, 1956.

Sthūlibhadra-phāgu by Jinapadma Sūri and *Neminātha-phāgu* by Rājaśekhara Sūri are edited by J.B. Sandesara in *Pracīna-phāgu-sangraha,* II (1952-53), pp. 277 ff. with a critical study; re-published in *Pracīna-phāgu-sangraha,* Baroda 1955, pp. 3-11. The same editor adds two other *Neminātha-phāgus.* both of them composed by Kṛṣṇārsiya Jayasiṁha Sūri.

2nd edition of *Sthūlibhadra-phāgu* by Jinapadma Sūri published by H. C. Bhayani in *Śrī Forbes gujarātī sabhā granthāvalī,* Bombay V. S. 2011, with a lexicon and a translation into modern Gujarātī. In the same volume the editor includes the *Revantagiri-rāsu* by Vinayasena Sūri and the *Neminātha-catuspadikā* by Vinayacandra Sūri.

life in her turn; this is so in the *Neminātha-catuṣpadikā*, mentioned above. Although the theme of this legend hardly seems compatible with the specific features of the *phāgu* just examined, the poet Rājaśekhara Sūri was able to adapt it to his needs. The *Nemināttha-phāgu* gives a lengthy description of the charms of spring and the beauty of the two heroes, the fiancée's dazzling procession and Rājimatī's toilet and jewels (stanzas 1-21). The tragic, austere ending of the episode is dealt with briefly in the last six stanzas, and the Jain author, in extolling Rājimati's beauty, is mainly concerned with emphasizing the greatness of Nemi's sacrifice. Rājimatī's long wait and sufferings are not even mentioned. The author merely states that Nemi remained deaf to her supplications.

Although all popular tradition associates the *viraha* theme with the pathetic character of Rājimatī, the fiancée abandoned on her wedding day, it is not even touched upon in Rājaśekhara Sūri's *Nemināttha-phāgu*.[39] The author's aim was to make the Neminātha legend into a *phāgu* with a Jain ending; hence he omitted the tragic element, Rājimatī's *viraha*, and concentrated on brilliant descriptions: the beauties of spring and the heroine's charms and sumptuous toilet, with the result that the gay note characteristic of the *phāgu* predominates almost up to the end, when it finally gives way to an edifying conclusion.

The *Sirī Thūlibhaddu phāgu* [*Śrī Sthūlibhadra phāgu*] composed by another Jain poet, Jinapadma Sūri (c. 1330) is considered to be the oldest known *phāgu*. It is a short poem—27 stanzas—in praise of Sthūlibhadra, a famous character in Jain hagiography (see Part II, Specimen VIII).

According to legend, Sthūlibhadra, son of the Rajah of Pātaliputra's minister, fell helplessly in love with the courtesan Kośā, so much so that he spent twelve consecutive years in her house. On becoming a minister in his turn, Sthūlibhadra renounces the

39. Compare for in instance another *Nemināttha-phāgu* on this theme, composed by the poet Ḍungar (late 15th/16th century) and published by Desai in *Jaina Yuga* varsa 5, p. 475; in spite of being called a "phāgu", this poem takes the form of a *viraha-bārahmāsā*, beginning with the month of Āṣāḍha and put into Rājimatī's mouth. A. Nahta (V.S. 2010) declares that he possesses a manuscript of this poem dated V.S. 1549, in 25 stanzas, and that the author is a certain "Kānha".

vanities of the world and receives the Jain *dīkṣā* from the hands of the *ācarya* Saṁbhūtivijaya. In order to test his novice's virtue, the guru sends him to spend a whole *caturmāsya*, i.e. the four months of the rainy season (during which a monk is forbidden to travel) in Kośā's house...The heroic Sthūlibhadra resists Kośā's charms and supplications and emerges from the test victorious; he even instructs Kośā in the ways of detachment and she in her turn embraces the ascetic way of life.

The poem is divided into 7 *bhāsa*s or groups of stanzas, introduced by one couplet briefly indicating the subject, i.e. the praise of the virtues of the *muni* Sthūlibhadra "in *phāgu* form".

bhāsa 1 : arrival of Sthūlibhadra at Kośā's house.

bhāsa 2 : the rainy season and its effects on the separated lovers.

*bhāsa*s 3 & 4 : Kośā's sumptuous toilet and description of her beauty.

*bhāsa*s 5 & 6 : dialogue between Sthūlibhadra and Kośā; Sthūlibhadra repulses Kośā.

bhasa 7 : Sthūlibhadra's victory and Kośā's conversion. Eulogy of Sthūlibhadra's heroism.

Jinapadma's *Sthūlibhadra-phāgu* moves even further away from the classic conception of the *phāgu* than does Rājaśekhara's *Neminātha-phāgu* : spring is not mentioned at all, only the rainy season (*caturmāsya*) and there is no description of *saṁyoga-śṛṅgāra*. And the story does not end with the reunion of the lovers, but with their final separation, i.e. with their renunciation of human love, when the heroine also embraces the ascetic life (as in the Jain legend of Neminātha and Rājimatī). However, the central part of the poem (*bhāsa*s 3 and 4) consists of a lively, sensual description of the heroine's toilet and beauty, in keeping with the *phāgu* tradition; there is no account of the heroine's *viraha*, just one brief allusion to a *virahiṇi* in *bhāsa* 2, describing the rainy season.

Although the action takes place during the rainy season, the first line indicates that this is a *phāgu*, and the last, in conclusion, that this *phāgu* is intended to be played and sung in the month of Caitra, i.e. in spring:

kharataragacchi jinapadamasūri kiü phāgu ramevaü
khela nācaiṁ caitramāsi rangihi gavevaü

"May this *phāgu*, composed by Jinapadma Sūri, of the Kharatara branch, please everyone
And may it be sung, played and danced in the month of Caitra, in great jollity."

In contrast, the first line of the third stanza refers to the time when the events actually take place, i.e. the four months of the rainy season:

varisalaī caumāsa-mahi sāhū gahagahiyā
liyaï abhiggai guruha pāsi niya-guṇa-mahamahiyā

"During the "four months" [of the rainy season], the holy men, joyful,
Are accustomed to come and take the *abhigraha* with their guru, they who are full of virtue..."

The description of the rainy season takes up the whole of *bhāsa* 2 (stanzas 6-9) and follows the folk-song style, with onomatopeia imitating the noise of the rain and with characteristic allusions to the *virahiṇi*, the clouds (of the month of Āṣāḍha) and the travellers' return, but Kośā is not named:

jhirimiri jhirimiri e meha varisante
khalahala khalahala khalahala e vāhala vahante
jhaba jhaba jhaba jhaba e vījuliya khabakkaï
tharahara tharahara tharahara e virahiṇī-manu kampaï

But there is no account of Kośā's *viraha*, and we move on at once to a description of her toilet and finery, a common theme in the *phāgu*, but one which never occurs in the *caumāsā* or the *viraha-bārahmāsā*.

H.C. Bhayani[40] has noted several metrical peculiarities in this short poem: out of the 7 *bhāsa*s composing it, nos. 1-5 are regularly formed of an equal number of stanzas. i.e. 3 *kaḍi*s or couplets in the *roḷā* metre followed by a *dohā*; but the last two *bhāsa*s are irregular: no. 6 has only 2 *kaḍī*s instead of 3; no. 7 has 3 *kaḍī*s but no *dohā*. The same author points out that the *dohā*

40. In a short introduction to his edition of the *Sthūlibhadra-phāgu*, cf. note 38 above.

which acts as an introduction is a *mukkhabandha* which is set apart from the 7 *bhāsas*. These peculiarities are indicative of the hybrid nature of the work, which is a *caumāsā* arranged as a *phāgu* and fitted with an edifying conclusion. Like the *Bārah navaü* discussed above, the poem is dedicated to the praise of a Jain monk, but whereas the *Bārah navaü* was modelled on the didactic *bārahmāsā*, the *Sthūlibhadra-phāgu* seems to owe its shape to an old *caumāsā* (most probably a Kośā-*caumāsā*).

The fact that so many *bārahmāsās* have been produced by Jain authors, such as the *Neminātha-catuṣpadikā* (see Part II, Specimen VII) on the theme of Rājimatī's *viraha*, shows that the Jain *munis* were quick to use *viraha-gītas* of the *caumāsā* or *bārahmāsā* type to disseminate their ascetic teaching, and the change from *viraha* to *vairāgya*, i.e. from a lament for solitude to an attitude of contempt for the world and its fleeting joys, occurs as a natural development. But here, in the *Sthūlibhadra-phāgu*, interest is transferred from the heroine, Kośā, to the hero, Sthūlibhadra (whose strength of mind is such that he remains unmoved by the courtesan Kośā's beauty and dazzling finery), and the whole is presented as an entertainment of the *phāgu* type, although the action takes place during the *caturmāsya*. The fact that Jain *munis* started composing *phāgus* as early as the 14th century to promote their ascetic view of life reveals how popular this kind of composition must have been in the provinces of Western India;[41] the *Sthūlibhadra-phāgu* also suggests that songs of the *caumāsā* type, having Kośā, sorrowing for Sthūlibhadra, as heroine, were already in existence.

e. *Caumāsā* and *viraha-gīta*

The *caumāsā* (*caturmāsya*), a rain song on the *viraha* theme of a young woman left alone, is the oldest lyric type known in the

41. The term *phāgu* seem to have evolved in the same way as *rāso*, *rāsa* (cf. notes 34 and 35, above). The association with the spring game of Holī has gradually faded and the word *phāgu* has come to mean any sort of lyrical composition on a romantic theme, usually including a variety of metres. Poems composed in one metre, or one main metre, are usually called by the name of this metre: *rās* (*rāsaka*), *dohā* (*dodhaka*), *caupāī* (*chatuṣpadikā*) (cf. *Neminātha-catuṣpadikā*). Thus *bārahmāsās* are found under the name of *Neminātha-rāsa*, *Nemināthaphāgu* and *Neminātha-caupāī*. A Nahta (V.S. 2010) mentions a *Neminātha bārahmāsā rāso* composed in the second half of the 14th century V.S. in OG by the poet "Palhaṇu".

written literature of the Indo-Aryan languages. Grierson remarks that many of the fragments collected by Hāḷa in the *Sattasāī* seem to have been borrowed from Prākrit poems of this kind. The same genre is in evidence in the oldest Sanskrit *dūta-kāvyas*, the *Ghaṭakarpara-kāvya* and Kālidāsa's *Meghadūta*.[42] Songs of the kind are still plentiful today in the oral literature of the villages in Northern India.[43]

A *caumāsā* usually begins with a reference to the month of Āṣāḍha and its dark skies, the husband himself often being compared or identified with the beneficent cloud. Sometimes the *caumāsā* begins with Śrāvaṇa, which is the month when the rain actually starts to fall in Northern and North-Western India; this last type, called a *Śāvan*, is a variety of *caumāsā*. The husband's return is rarely mentioned at the end of a *caumāsā* : the *viraha* theme is the only one, and it is always put into the mouth of a woman; the roles are never reversed.

This is an essentially lyrical type in the pathetic or elegiac mode, in which the description of the rainy season is always combined with the *virahiṇī's* laments. Only in the popular type of *caumāsā* are the two themes found together, inextricably mingled. While the *viraha-bārahmāsā* represents the main but not the only form of *bārahmāsā* (a form with indeterminate content, as we have seen), there is no example of a *caumāsā* which is not a *viraha-caumāsā*. The conjunction of the descriptive element with the lyric element is not the result of chance or evolution: this is clearly the case of primitive type of women's folk-song. Introducing a *caumāsā* sung by the high-caste women of a Bihar village, W.G. Archer stresses this constant association of rain with *viraha* :

"The theme of the cycle is sexual frustration, a theme which almost all folk-poetry in India connects with the rains".[44]

Indeed the hero whose absence the *virahiṇī* is bewailing nearly

42. Cf. note 8, above.

43. Cf. note 9, above.

44. W. G. Archer, *Seasonal Songs of the Patna District*, Man in India, Vol. XXII, 1942, p. 232. Archer quotes a line from one of these songs, where the young woman says:

"My husband is a *cloud* in another land".

always matches the clouds, being a "dark-complexioned Yādao [Yādava]", Kṛṣṇa or Nemi. References to clouds and rain recur like a leit-motiv in all *sandeśa* ("messages") literature on the theme of the wife's *viraha*, in Apabhraṁśa and OG. Thus the ancient ballad *Ḍholā-Mārū-rā Dūhā* in Old Rājasthānī includes many fragments of those rain songs, and also songs of the month of Kārttika, known as *akṣepokti*, where a wife tries to prevent her husband from leaving after the rains, i.e. in the month of Kārttika.[45]

In contrast to the *bārahmāsā*, the *caumāsā* seems always to have been an essentially oral village composition, never having developed to the same extent as *bārahmāsā*s and *phāgu*s in Indo-Aryan written vernacular literatures : on the one hand the *caumāsā* was a purely lyric type, unsuitable for preaching; on the other it was a women's song, probably composed by illiterate villagers. However, compilations of vishnuite *pada*s in Bengal include several interesting specimens of *caumāsā*s on the theme of Rādhā's *viṛaha* for Krishna; the oldest is the *caumāsā* included in Baḍu Caṇḍīdās's *Śrīkṛṣṇakīrtana*.[46] This is a long *vijaya-kāvya*, dealing with the "conquest" (*vijaya*) of the *gopi* Rādhā by Kṛṣṇa. Kṛṣṇa himself is not portrayed very sympathetically, but Rādhā is a model of faithfulness and tenderness. The sources of the work are various but the puranic element seems to be of less significance than the folklore element. A large number of village songs are incorporated, thanks to which this interesting specimen of a *caumāsā* in Old Bengali has been preserved.

In Bengal, we find *caumāsā*s in the *Padābali* of Jñāndās, a contemporary of Govindadās (late 16th century) who imitated

45. Cf. Ch. Vaudeville, *Ḍholā-Mārū-rāDūhā*, Institut Francais d'Indologie, Pondichery, 1963, Introd. pp. 48 ff. and Appendix A, on the use of rain songs in the *Ḍholā-Mārū*.

The type of Kārttika song known as *akṣepokti* lends itself to development into a *bārahmāsā*; cf. *Rāyā Candra Sūri guru bārahmāsā,* published in *Aitihāsika rāsa-sangraha* by Vijaya Dharma Sūri (Bhavnagar, 1917) and analyzed by Tessitori in IA. Vol. XLVI, 1917, p. 134: Rajah Candra's sister describes to him the different beauties and pleasures of the twelve months of the year in order to dissuade him from taking the Jain *dīkṣā*. But this is not a *viraha-bārahmāsā*.

46. Cf. Part II, Specimen II.

the style of Caṇḍīdās. The large collection of vishnuite *padas*, *Padakalpataru* compiled at the beginning of the 18th century by Vaishnavadās (alias Gokulananda Sen), also contains some. However, in Bengali literature after Caitanya, Rādhā's *viraha* for Kṛṣṇa tends to be expressed in *bārahmāsā* rather than *caumāsā* form, the latter already appearing as an archaic type of composition. The *bāromāsis* on the theme of Rādhā's *viraha* are found in all collections of vishnuite *padas* in Bengali among the poems grouped under the name of *biraha-kahini.*

The *caumāsā* lends itself uneasily to dramatization. Rādhā's *caumāsā* in the *Śrīkṛṣṇakīrtana* stays as a simple song among many others, the whole making up the last part of the work, known as *Rādhā-viraha*. The only example of a *caumāsā* where a dramatic element is introduced is the *Sthūḷibhadra-phāgu* of Jinapadma Sūri, analyzed above (pp. 24-27), where the Jain author presents an unusual situation likely to strike the imagination of his listeners: the faithless lover is not in a distant country, he is present in the *virahiṇī*'s house—present in body but not in mind.

The lyric, descriptive type of the *viraha-bārahmāsā* is thrown into perspective by the primitive type of the *caumāsā*, of which it may simply be an enlargement. The *caumāsā* is always a pure *viraha-gīta* : the *virahiṇī* remains anonymous and the circumstances of the separation are not mentioned. But it only needs the imagination to be put to work on the circumstances of the lovers' or spouses' separation or the events which could have brought it about for the *caumāsā* to turn quite naturally into a *barahmāsā*. It is inconceivable that the wandering husband should have left home at the beginning of the rainy season, therefore he must have departed in the month of Kārttika the year before, hence the wife's *viraha* will have lasted for a whole year. The four months of the rainy season thus represent the last four months of her test, when the strain is even greater than during the other eight.[47]

47. This is precisely the situation described in the introduction to Kalidāsa's *Meghadūta* (stanza 2), in spite of the reversal of the male-female roles. The Yakṣa of the *Meghadūta* has been separated from his beloved for eight months already, but it at the sight of the clouds of the

In principle, a *viraha-bārahmāsā* should begin with the husband's departure, in the month of Kārttika, which marks the end of the rainy season and the beginning of the dry season, favourable for trading or warrior expeditions and for ascetic pilgrimages. This is true of Rājimatī's *bārahmāsā* included in the *Bīsaldev-rās*.[48] More often, however, this is not the case: in spite of the resemblance, most old *viraha-bārahmāsā*s begin with a description of the rainy season. This occurs in the *bārahmāsā*s of Sūfī poets in Avadhī, inspired by folk literature: in Mullā Dāūd's *Candāyan* (14th century) the *bārahmāsā* of Mainā, the neglected wife of Lorik, begins in the month of Śāvan (*śrāvaṇa* also being the name of a rain song, see above, p. 19); in Muhammad Jāyasī's *Padmāvat*, the *bārahmāsā* of Nāgamatī, the neglected wife of Ratansen, begins in Āṣāḍha, "month of clouds", and the four months of the rainy season are treated in much the same way, with the enumeration of the *nakṣatra*s (constellations) which preside over the rainy months; there is no mention of *nakṣatra*s for the eight other months.[49] Rājal's *bārahmāsā* in the *Neminātha-catuṣpadikā* also begins with the month of Āṣāḍha.[50] In contrast, *bārahmāsā*s with an enumerative or didactic content usually begin with the month of Caitra, the first month of spring and the first month of the year in modern times.[51]

It thus seems highly probable that the *viraha-bārahmāsā* has its roots in the primitive rain song; it is a lyric type, quite separate from the enumerative or didactic *bārahmāsā* studied earlier. In addition, when the *viraha-bārahmāsā* is compared with the *caumāsā* from which it has sprung, it becomes clear how the transition from song to ballad came about : the circumstances which gave rise to the *viraha* expressed in the song were imagined afterwards, being explained in a brief introductory stanza placed before the mention of the first month, and the

---

month of Āṣādha (or *nabhas*, "month of clouds") that he breaks into lamentations (cf. Ch. Vaudeville, *A Note on the Ghaṭakarpara and the Meghadūta*, Baroda, 1959, v. supra n.8.)

48. Cf. Part II, Specimen IV.
49. Cf. Part II, Specimen V.
50. Cf. Part II, Specimen VII.
51. Cf. Part II, Specimen VI.

eight other months are added after the fourth month of the *caumāsā*; after which the introductory stanza may be repeated, as in the *Nemināthа-catuṣpadikā*,[52] or another conclusion found, sometimes the return of the husband, as in the *Bīsaldev-rās*.[53] This explains why the name of the hero and heroine do not appear in the *bārahmāsā* itself, but only in the introduction or the conclusion, and also why the same *bārahmāsā* may be used in different contexts, spoken by different heroines.[54] Even when it is included in a narrative work, the *viraha-bārahmāsā* always remains a short, independent lyric poem, like the *caumāsā* of which it is simply a development.

The popularity of the "versatile" form of the *bārahmāsā* certainly helped the *caumāsā* to develop into a *viraha-bārahmāsā*, but it is the dependence of the latter on the former which provides a reason for the special features of the type, as compared with other types of *bārahmāsā*. This line of descent also explains the similarities between the *viraha-bārāhmāsā* and certain types of *phāgu* or *rāsa*, which were themselves influenced by the old *caturmāsya*. The enormous popularity of the *viraha-bārahmāsā* in all Indo-Aryan literatures from the 14th century onwards is also due to its ancestry: without the lyrical inspiration, the richness of emotion and the evocative power which give village rain songs their charm, the *bārahmāsā* would have remained a didactic, fairly prosaic genre. It is through the *viraha-bārahmāsā* that the old rain song has been raised to the rank of a lyric

52. Cf. Part II, Specimen VII.

53. Cf. Part II, Specimen IV, "Rājimatī-Bārahmāsā"; the name "Rājal", found in other versions of the *Bīsaldev-rās*, seems to be a variant of the same name.

54. In *viraha-bārahmāsa*s in OG and Avadhi, the *virahiṇī* is often called *dhana*, "young woman, wife"; sometimes she calls her husband *dhanī* and sometimes she bestows various epithets on him, flattering or otherwise, which often refer to his wanderings. The proper names of the two protagonists only appear in the introduction and the conclusion, the song itself keeping to anonymity. Whether the heroine is Mainā languishing for Lorik, Rājal for Bīsaldev, or Rājimatī for Neminātha, or again Rādhā for Kṛṣṇa the sentiments expressed and the pathetic tone are the same. The dramatic or narrative element is in juxtaposition to the *viraha-bārahmāsā*.

genre and found a place in all written literatures of Northern India.

f. Western origin of the *viraha-bārahmāsā.*

A husband's seasonal wanderings are the inevitable background to the *caumāsā* and the *viraha-bārahmāsā*. These rain songs on the *viraha* theme, always female, must have materialized spontaneously in a society where the man is absent from the village for a large part of the year, and only the woman leads a settled life. In a pastoral, trading or warrior society, the rainy season which brings the men back home is the time that the women bless and long for. Āṣāḍha, "month of clouds", heralding the rain, is the month of return and reunion. It is also the time when the roof of the house is repaired to withstand the coming rains. If the husband is late returning, the wife is seized with anxiety and bursts into lamentations, or else sends a desperate message to her husband. It is to this situation that several *gāthā*s of Hāla's *Sattasāī* refer,[55] also an old *dohā* (*dodhaka*) found in Merutunga Ācārya's *Prabandhacintāmaṇi* :

"Munja, the rope has fallen, you do not see it, mean wretch! The clouds of Āṣāḍha are roaring, the ground will now be slimy."[56]

Trading and soldiering are traditional occupations for a large section of the populations of the Western provinces, especially in Gujarat and Rajasthan. Pastoral tribes are also numerous in North-West India, from Saurashtra to the Braj country and Bundelkhand. It is probable that this type of song developed markedly in the great nomad or semi-nomad tribe of the Jādons (Yādava), a turbulent race of pastors, caravaneers and soldiers.

Indeed, in the west, the hero for whom the *virahiṇī* is pining is usually a merchant held up by his trading activities in a foreign country, or an *ulagānā*, in the service of a distant lord. The OG word *ulagānā* is a suffixed form of the Pr.-Ap. *oluggo* which the grammarian Hemachandra interprets as *sevaka*, *niśchāya* and

55. Cf. *Gāthā-Saptasatī* (ed. Kāvyamālā, I, 29; IV, 15; VI, 37; VII, 36; VII, 73, 94.

56. *Prabandhacintāmaṇi* by Merutunga Ācarya; English translation by C. H. Tawney, Calcutta 1899, p. 31.

nisthāma : "servant", "shadowless one", "homeless one".[57] The Apabhraṁśa dictionary *Paia-sadda-mahavaṇṇo* only gives the first meaning and interprets *olaggi* as *sevā, cakarī* : "service".[58] The literal meaning of *ulagānā* would thus be "servant", in the sense of a vassal or a mercenary in a prince's service, a frequent profession among the warrior castes of Rajasthan, the "Rajputs". The term is apt for a mercenary soldier, vowed to a wandering life governed by the campaigns waged by his lord, and it seems logical to interpret it in this way in the first stanza of the *Rājimatī-bārahmāsā* (see Part II, Specimen IV). However, in this case, the hero cannot be identified with Rajah Bīsaldev of the Chauhān dynasty or with any other Rajah mentioned in Rajput chronicles.

In Jain *viraha-bārahmāsā*s in OG, the hero is almost always the Yādava Prince Nemināthа, beloved of Rājal or Rājimatī, daughter of the Yādava King Ugrasena, while in the East, in Bihar and Bengal, the hero is Prince Kṛṣṇa, lover of the *gopī* Rādhā.

Zbavitel stresses the fact that, in modern *viraha-bārahmāsā*s in Bengali, the *virahiṇī*'s husband is invariably represented as a merchant, and notes in this context :

> "And yet it is immediately obvious that the economic and social conditions which gave rise to this "story" have changed considerably, that the Bengali merchants no longer leave their homes for a full year to wander over land and sea, leaving their longing wives at home".[59]

It is certain that in Bengal the sedentary and farming element is much greater than the nomad element, not only in number, but also in social standing. But the fact is not new : D. C. Sen notes that in old Bengal the merchant castes, in spite of their riches, never enjoyed much prestige.[60] And in Bengal, as elsewhere, the *viraha-bārahmāsā* does not seem much in favour among the merchant castes. But it is widespread among all castes of sedentary farmers, traditionally suspicious of the *banya*, who

57. *Deśīnāmamālā* I, 164.
58. *Paia-sadda-mahavaṇṇo*, 2nd edition, 1962, p. 201.
59. Zbavitel, op, cit., 1961, p. 595.
60. D. C. Sen, op. cit., p. 518.

often is not a local man but comes from the western provinces, Marvar in particular. In the eastern provinces, the Marvari merchant is as unpopular as he is powerful. The fact that the pathetic *virahiṇī*'s beloved is often a merchant, or at least a wanderer, cannot be explained by any prestige that a merchant might have in that society, but rather by the influence of a different oral literature : that of the pastoral tribes, from the west, and in particular the innumerable Yādavas or Jādons who spread their legends and songs over the whole of Northern India. It is certainly no accident that the pastor-god Kṛṣṇa, the Yādava hero, is almost invariably associated with the Bengali *biraha-kahinī*s, while in the west the *viraha-bārahmāsā*s in OG are concerned with Nemi, another Yādava hero and Krishna's cousin. In addition, specimens in OG are clearly older than Bengali *bāromāsī*s on the *viraha* theme. Indeed, Bengal is the only province where the first *bārahmāsā*s found in written literature belong to the didactic type and not the *viraha-bārahmāsā* type.

The hypothesis of the western origin of the *caumāsā* and *viraha-bārahmāsā* is validated by certain peculiarities of language picked out by Zbavitel in Bengali *baromāsī*s. Wondering why the month of Phālgun goes hand in hand with the phrase *phāgu* (or *phāguyā*) *khele rājā*, "the princes play at *phāgu*", the author suggests the explanation that the name of the month, *phālguna*, resembles the word *phāgu*.[61] But *phāg* or *phāgu* (Ap. *phaggu*) is the Rājasthānī-Gujarātī name for the spring festival in which people throw red powder (Skt. *phalguh* "red") at each other, a festival better known in the eastern provinces under the name of Holī. The repeated use of the word *phāgu* with the final vowel *u* instead of the Bengali *phāg*(*a*) or *holī*, suggests that it is borrowed from a western language.

Another anomaly noticed by Zbavitel in Bengali *baromāsī*s is the expression *pauṣa andhakāra*. Why should the month of Pauṣa (*pus* = December/January) be qualified as "dark"? The author notes that the word *pauṣa* is written in many different ways in these poems, with "quite fantastic" variations, and that it is even replaced sometimes by the word *puṣpa* (flower), which

61. Zbavitel, op. cit., p. 597.

gives the inexplicable combination of *puṣpa-andhakāra* ! Obviously the expression *pauṣa andhakāra*, hallowed by use, soon ceased to be understood, for the month of *pus*, in Bengal, has nothing dark about it, being a time of brilliant sunshine. The meaning emerges from a study of *viraha-bārahmāsā*s in Rājasthānī and Gujarātī, in which the dark days are naturally those of the rainy season (Ap. *pāvasa*, OG *paüs*, *paüs*, G. *pos*). The expression *pauṣa andhakāra* must have been lifted straight from western models, but the word *paüs*, incomprehensible in Bengal, soon changed into *paus* (*pūs*), meaning the first month of the cold season; the expression *paüṣa andhakāra*, transformed into *paus andhakār*, was thus used as it stood in the description of this month. It is interesting to compare this *paus andhakār* with a line of Rādhā's *caumāsā* in the *Śrīkṛṣṇakīrtana*, where the lack of light is attributed, quite naturally, to the nights of the month of Bhādon, the third month of the rainy season :

bhādar māse ahoniśi andhakāre...
"In the month of Bhādon, it is dark day and night..."

5. THE "RELIGIOUS" *BĀRAHMĀSĀ*

The concept of the "religious *bārahmāsā* has already been examined. If *bārahmāsā*s listing the religious festivals during the twelve months of the year, or even the twelve ways of worshipping a god, can be considered "religious", the genre is very widely represented in all oral vernacular literatures; but it rarely appears in written literature in this primitive form.[62] However, the *bārahmāsā* was a useful vehicle for dispensing different kinds of teaching to a peasant audience, and because of its popularity preachers of various persuasions made use of it. As for the lyric type of *viraha-bārahmāsā* with its intense nostalgia, it had the power to turn people's hearts away from earthly affections. It is not surprising, therefore, to see both types widely used by folk preachers—Jains, Nāth-yogīs, Sūfīs and Sants.

62. The anonymous *bārahmāsā* in Marāṭhi given in Part II (Specimen VI) is of the same type : it is mainly a list of festivals and rites of the Hindu year.

a. The Jain *bārahmāsā*

The Jain preachers seem to have been the first to use the *bārahmāsā* to disseminate moral and religious teaching; several old specimens of Jain *bārahmāsā*s have come down to us, written in vulgar Apabhraṁśa (*grāmya apabhraṁśa*) or in old Gujarātī. Many works of this type are probably still waiting to be discovered in the *jaina bhaṇḍār* (collections of Jain manuscripts) in Gujarat and Rajasthan.

The first Jain *bārahmāsā*s may have been simple sermons, or panegyrics of Jain saints in *bārahmāsā* form. The strange *Bārah navaü* analyzed above (pp. 18-19) suggests the existence of *bārahmāsā*s of this type, and the fact that fragments of *viraha-gīta*s are incorporated in the panegyric of Dharam Sūri indicates that the *viraha bārahmāsā* was already popular at that time among the Jains. But the odd, hybrid nature of this poem is perhaps due to successive interpolations, and the text appears too corrupt for it to be dated.

The *viraha-bārahmāsā* was used by Jain *muni*s following a more or less invariable pattern : some event, which is not always described, since it would already be known, leads the hero to renounce the world and take the Jain *dīkṣā*; the heroine—lover, fiancée or young wife—pines for twelve months in the agonies of *viraha* and at last decides to follow the hero in the ascetic life. The moral of the story is not expressed directly but simply suggested: all human attachment is evil and the cause of endless suffering; the only remedy for lovesickness is total detachment and renunciation of the world. The deep-seated pessimism of the Jains and their eagerness to convince common mortals of the vanity of human affections explains these authors' predilection for love stories with an unhappy ending: finishing not with the reunion of the separated lovers but with irremediable separation and disillusionment. The pathetic tone of the rain song was ideal for their purposes; the *viraha* thus seems to have been the Jain preacher's natural ally. The oldest specimen of a Jain *viraha-bārahmāsā* is Vinayachandra Sūri's *Neminātha-catuṣpadikā*, mentioned above (see p. 13 and n. 27 and Part II, Specimen VII).

b. The Sūfī *bārahmāsā*

From the second half of the 14th century, the Sūfī poets of

Oudh also began composing *viraha bārahmāsās*, in Avadhī. These are not short independent poems like the Jain works in OG, but often long lyrical pieces included in *premākhyāns*, love-stories with an allegorical meaning, in the style of the Persian *mathnavīs*. The two oldest *mathnavīs* in Avadhī, Mullā Dāūd's *Candāyan*, mentioned above, and Qutban's *Mṛgavatī* each contain a *viraha-bārahmāsā*. The most polished specimen of the kind, in all Indian literatures, is without doubt Nāgamatī's famous *bārahmāsā* in Muhammad Jāyasī's *Padmāvat*.[63]

The Sūfī poets' liking for *viraha-bārahmāsās*, and more especially for stories where the *viraha* ends with the hero's death, is understandable in view of their own particular conception of love. Sūfī writers in Avadhī see in *viraha* (or *viraha-prema*) the equivalent of the Persian *'ishq* : an inextinguishable fire, a mortal torment consuming those whom it possesses, bearing them inexorably towards death.[64] Like *'ishq*, *viraha* is divine in origin and nature, the sole path which leads the soul of the *mushāqin* (the equivalent of the Hindī *sādhaka*) to a state of vision or to absorption, after death, into supreme Beauty.

While interpreting the *viraha* as the equivalent of *'ishq*, Sūfī writers have, however, introduced a new and typical element into the story : it is the hero rather than the heroine who is prey to the torture of *viraha*; the *virahiṇī* of Hindu tradition becomes a *virahī* in Sūfī works. This reversal of the situation obviously arises from the equivalence between *viraha* and *'ishq*, leading to the further equivalence between *virahī* and *mushāqin*. However, the rain song tradition, and hence the tradition of the *viraha-bārahmāsā* as a female song, was too old and well-established for Sūfī writers to be able to make the transposition easily. While the main heroine of Sūfī *mathnavīs* symbolises divine Beauty for which the hero is pining in the torments of *viraha*, it is a secondary heroine, usually the hero's first wife, who appears as the traditional *virahiṇī* and sings the *viraha-bārahmāsā*; thus the Muslim authors of *mathnavīs* in Avadhī respect the Hindu tradition of the *viraha bārahmāsā* in attributing the song

63. Cf. Part II, Specimen V.

64. Cf. Ch. Vaudeville, *La conception de l'amour divin dans la Padmāvat de M. Jayasī, virah* et *'ishq*, JA 1963, pp. 351 ff.

to a neglected wife. Nevertheless, there is at least one example of a *viraha bārahmāsā* put into the mouth of a male character : Majnūn's *bārahmāsā* in Bāhrām Khān's *Laylī Majnū*, in Bengali; but this is a much later work and the legend is borrowed from Arabic folklore, which almost always attributes the torments of unhappy love to the hero.

*Bārahmāsā*s found in *mathnavī*s in Avadhī are noteworthy for their greater degree of development and also their flamboyant style and mystic exaltation. *Viraha* is described as a devouring fire, kindled in the heart of the *virahiṇī*, which spreads to the whole universe and threatens to reduce it to cinders—as in Nāgamatī's *bārahmāsā* included by Jāyasī in the *Padmāvat*, stanza 355 :

"Virah, as a Hanumān, rises with a roar—
He sets my whole body on fire like another Lankā !"

But here there is no moralizing epilogue as in the Jain *bārahmāsā*s; the *viraha bārahmāsā* of the neglected wife usually leads to a turning-point in the story: the forgetful husband returns to the *virahiṇī* and grants her, at least temporarily, the favour of his presence.

A certain number of independent *bārahmāsā*s occur from the time of Akbar onwards, composed by Hindu and in particular by Muslim writers. Garcin de Tassy mentions some in his *Histoire de la littérature hindouie et hindoustanie.*[65] A Nahta

65. In H.L.H.H., Garcin de Tassy refers to several *bārahmāsā*s composed in the 18th and 19th centuries by Hindu poets (e.g. the *Rācamandra kī bārahmāsā* of the poet Bhavanī, printed at Fatehgarh in 1868, cf. H.L.H.H. Vol. I, p. 329) and also to a certain number of *bārahmāsā*s composed in "Hindustani", i.e. Urdu, by Muslim poets, such as the *Bikat kahāni* of Kammal Shāh Muhāmmad Afzal of Allahabad (H.L.H.H. I, p. 139). Garcin also refers to an interesting *Dvāzda mānsa* ("12 months" in Persian), a *mathnavī* 28 pages long divided into 12 short songs, the manuscript of which is preserved at the Bibliothèque Impériale (Nationale) in Paris. Garcin de Tassy (H.L.H.H. II, pp. 95 ff.) gives several fragments of the "Bārahmāsā" of the Muslim poet Mirzā Kazīn 'Ali Jawān, of Delhi (late 18th/early 19th century). This poem also bears the title of *Dastūr-i Hind* ("Customs of India") and describes the festivals and customs of the Hindus and Muslims of Northern India. However, the extracts given by Garcin de Tassy show that this is not a *bārahmāsā* but a *ṣaḍ-ṛtu-varṇana*, "description of the six seasons".

notes that *bārahmāsā*s composed by Hindus do not usually attain any great length, consisting of 25 to 30 stanzas, while Muslim *bārahmāsā*s tend to turn into allegorical or philosophical dissertations.[66] The *bārahmāsā* in 122 stanzas by the 18th century poet Hamḍa Qāzī is a long poem in praise of "Viraha". It begins with an eulogy to the Creator who "kindled Viraha's lamp" to light the heart of man; then follows the actual *viraha bārahmāsā*, describing the sufferings of a *virahiṇī* during the twelve months of the year. The epilogue is unexpected and symbolic : thanks to Viraha, the neglected wife discovers the divine Husband in her own house (in her soul). Here the *viraha-bārahmāsā* is included in a longer poem of the didactic type. The *viraha* theme is used for religious ends, but different ones to those pursued by the Jain *muni*s. In both cases the *viraha* is represented as unbearable torment, but whereas the Jain *muni* aims to put an end to the torment by renouncing the attachment which is the cause of it, the Sūfī considers that the torment in itself is holy, since it comes from God and leads to union with Him.

The fact that Indian Muslim poets look upon the *viraha* as equivalent to *'ishq* explains why they almost always stay within the confines of the *viraha-bārahmāsā*. Zbavitel, however, draws attention to a few late *bārahmāsā*s composed by Muslim poets in Bengali, where one of the characters bewails the loss of a father, brother or son; this seems to be a form derived from the traditional *viraha-bārahmāsā*.

c. The Hindu bhakta *bārahmāsā*

On the whole, few Hindu *smārta* poets have used the *bārahmāsā* for religious teaching purposes. However, there are poems of the "religious *bārahmāsā*" type in old Bengali listing the ritual acts to be performed before various deities throughout the twelve months of the year. The oldest *bārahmāsā* of this type is included in Vipradās's *Mānasa-maṅgal*[67]; other *Mānasa-maṅgal*s contain *bārahmāsā*s of the same type and various

66. Such as the *bārahmāsā*s composed by the poets Bullā Shāh, Hamḍa Qāzī, Muhāmmad Puramahī Ahmad Khairā Shāh and several others.

67. See above, p. 10.

*Caṇḍī-mangal*s as well. The use of *bārahmāsā*s for sermons thus seems to have been well-established in Bengali folk-literature from the end of the 15th century among devotees of local goddesses, in particular Caṇḍī, a manifestation of Durgā, and Manasā, goddess of serpents. Their purpose was to jog the memory of those who might otherwise forget their duties towards those goddesses, whose vengeance was particularly feared.

As regards the *biraha-kahinī*s included in collections of vishnuite *pada*s on the *viraha* theme of Rādhā deserted by Kṛṣṇa, they are pure *viraha-gīta*s with no sermon or allegory. Any mystical interpretation is left to the listener's imagination, insofar as he or she recognizes Rādhā and Kṛṣṇa as divine personages, or symbols of the human soul and of God. However, there is nothing in the song itself to point towards this interpretation; in the *biraha-kahinī*s, Rādhā expresses herself like a village maiden, a *mugdhā*, with a tender, faithful heart.

The poets of the ramaite and krisnaite *bhakti* who were writing in the 17th century in Avadhī and Braj do not seem to have used the traditional *bārahmāsā* form in their religious works to the glory of Rāma and Kṛṣṇa. It is true that tradition has credited them with such compositions, in fact a *bārahmāsā* attributed to Tulsīdās, the famous author of the Hindi *Rāmacaritamānasa*, was published in Allahabad in 1959. This poem is a sort of sermon in verse on the *Rāma-bhakti* in *bārahmāsā* form. It is of very doubtful authenticity.[68] Sūrdās, the greatest krishnaite poet in Braj, is also supposed to have written a *bārahmāsā* printed in Agra in the 19th century and mentioned by Garcin de Tassy.[69] There again the work is certainly apocryphal.

A. Nahta, in the article already mentioned (V. S. 2010) speaks of a *bārahmāsā* signed by the poet Gangā Kavi, a work found at the end of a manuscript of the Sūfī poet Qutban, a precedessor of Muhammad Jāyasī. According to Nahta, this is "the first

68. The publishers themselves (Belvedere Press), in a brief introduction, express doubts on the authenticity of this poem, found in the oral literature of the Bundelkhand transmitted "by a certain *bhakta*".

69. Garcin de Tassy, H.L.H.H., Vol. III, p. 183: "On a imprimé à Agra de format in-12 un Bārahmāsā écrit par Sūr-dās ou du moins attribué à ce célébre poète". ("A Bārahmāsā written by Sūr-Dās, or at least attributed to this famous poet, was printed in Agra in 12mo format.")

independent non-Jain *barahmāsā* known". Gangā Kavi was a secular poet at the imperial court of Akbar in the first half of the 16th century.

Muslim poets who used Bengali to recount the legends of Gorakhnāth and his disciple Gopī Candra (or Gopī Cand) did not fail to embellish their stories with *viraha-bārahmāsā*s; Sheikh Fayzulla's *Gorakṣa-vijaya* and Abdul Kunur Muhammad's Gopīcander (mentioned by Zbavitel, op. cit., p. 610) each include a *viraha-bārahmāsā*. Gopī Cand's mother, Mainā or Mainävatī, is a saint in the Gorakhnāthī tradition. This Mainā is the wife of "Lālan Shāh" or "Lorik" (manuscripts differ) and the heroine of the *Maināsat* attributed to the poet "Sādhan" by H. H. Dvivedi.[70] Mainā's *viraha-bārahmāsā* forms the main part of this poem.

d. The Sīkh and Sant *bārahmāsā*s

In spite of the extraordinary influence that the Gorakhnāthī yogīs exercised on low-caste Hindus and Muslims in the Middle Ages, as is shown by vernacular literatures from Hindi to Bengali, it does not seem that they themselves composed poems in *bārahmāsā* form. But, as a large part of this literature is lost or unexplored, it is not impossible that they did. In any case didactic *bārahmāsā*s were produced by Sikh and late "Sant" poets.

The sacred book of the Sīkhs, the *Guru-granth*, compiled by Guru Arjan (c. 1581) towards the end of the 16th century A.D., includes two *bārahmāsā*s known as *Bārā Māh* in Panjābī. The first is the work of the founder of the sect, Guru Nānak himself[71]: it is a didactic *bārahmāsā*, but one not lacking in inspiration or poetical skill. The second, by Guru Arjan[72], is rather prosaic. Nevertheless, the introduction contains an allusion to the pain of separation :

kirati karama ke vichūḍe kari kirapā melahu rāma

"O Rām ! Be merciful : unite with Thee those who are separated from Thee by their words or (evil) doings."

70. *Sādhan kṛt Maināsat*, ed. H.H.N. Dvivedi, Gwalior, 1959.

71. *Śrī guru grantha sāhib*, Amritsar, 1951, pp. 182-185. The *Bārā Māh* of Guru Nānak was translated into English by Kushwant Singh : *Hymns of Guru Nānak*, UNESCO; 1969, pp. 185-192.

72. Idem, pp. 133 ff., *Rāga Mājha, Bārā Māh.*

The oldest "Sant" poets (also called *nirguṇī* because they reject the concept of a visible divinity or one "imbued with qualities"), i.e. Nāmdev, Kabīr, Rāī-Dās and their contemporaries or direct successors, do not seem to have composed *bārahmāsā*s, although all of them made great use of the spiritual *viraha*, as a means of union with God. In his *dohā*s and *pada*s, Kabīr explains his own "*viraha* theology" and refers explicitly to rain songs on this theme.[73] Nevertheless no *viraha-bārahmāsā*s are found in the authentic works of Kabīr. Similarly, his main successor, the Muslim Dādū, who died in Ahmedabad in Gujarat in 1603, gave the *viraha* a place of honour in his *sādhanā* and borrowed freely from the rain songs, though without using the *bārahmāsā* form, and his disciples did the same.

It was later, in the 17th century, that the poets belonging to the Sant tradition took to using *bārahmāsā*s for spiritual teaching purposes : Sundardās, Dharaṇīdās, Gulāl Saheb and Bhīkhā Saheb composed long *bārahmāsā*s, on the *viraha* theme, sometimes didactic *bārahmāsā*s and sometimes allegorical ones, in a rather artificial style.[74] Compared with the early Sants, Sundardās and Dharaṇīdās are learned poets, employing allegory in the Sūfī style.

Dharaṇīdās's *bārahmāsā*[75], composed at the end of the 17th century, combines the characteristics of the didactic *bārahmāsā* and the allegorical *viraha-bārahmāsā*, inherited from the Sūfī poets. The poem is a dialogue between the *virahiṇī* and her *sakhī*. The description of the heroine's sufferings is interspersed with pious reflections on the vanity of the world. The *sakhī* plays the part of the (false) guru and urges the *virahiṇī* to set off in search of the missing Husband, but the *virahiṇī* tells her that the Husband will appear when and how he pleases. Finally

73. Cf. Ch. Vaudeville, *KABIR* I, Oxford, 1974: "The Sākhīs of Kabīr" 2.2 and *passim*:

"The Kunjha cranes cry plaintively in the sky
thunder and ponds are filled
But she whom her Lord has deserted
endures untold torments"

74. Cf. P. Chaturvedi, *Santa-kāvya*, op. cit., pp. 314-316.

75. Published in D. P. Sinha, op. cit., pp. 314-316.

the divine Husband returns and the faithful wife enjoys his presence "in her own house", i.e. she discovers his presence in her soul. The last three months of the *bārahmāsā* describe the joys of divine union.

The *bārahmāsā* survives as a literary form in the work of the last Sant poets into the middle of the 19th century; Palaṭūdās and Śiva Dayāl, founder of the modern sect of the Rādhāswāmīs, each composed a *bārahmāsā* towards the middle of the last century.[76]

Although the *bārahmāsā* now seems to have finished its long career as a literary genre, it is still very much alive in unwritten rural literatures. It continues to be a faithful echo of villagers' feelings. People are still composing *bārahmāsās*, and women in particular are still singing *viraha-bārahmāsās* about the pain of separation, for, as Kabīr declares, "Virah" is a King :

> "Do not abuse that Virah
> for Virah is a King :
> The body that contains not Virah
> is for ever a burning-ground![77]

76. D. P. Sinha recognizes the merits of the *bārahmāsā* of Palaṭū-Dās, which is a *viraha-bārahmāsā* with no pretentions to allegory. In contrast, the *bārahmāsā* of Shiva Dayāl appears as a cold dissertation in verse.

77. Translated in Vaudeville, KABIR : 1974, p. 164.

PART II

TEXTS AND TRANSLATIONS

from Indo-Aryan vernaculars*

*Unless indicated other wise, all the translations are by the Author. The original is in the Bengali and Gujarati scripts have been transliterated in the Nagari script.

I

DĀKER VACHANA

[Old Bengali]

1. In the month of Kārttik, one should eat *ol*,[1]
   in Mārga,[2] the *bel* fruit,[3]
   In Paush, *kānjī*,[4]
   in Māgh, mustard-oil.

2. In Phālgun, one should eat ginger,
   in Chaitra, bitter things,
   In Baisākh, *nīm*[5] and jute leaves.

3. In Jeṭh, one should have buttermilk,
   in Āshāṛh, curds,
   In Shrāvan, roasted grains,[6]
   in Bhādra, the *tāl* fruit.[7]

4. In Āshvin, one should eat cucumber,
   says Dākā :
   Such is my *Bārahmāsā*.

1. *ol* or *sūraṇ* : an edible root which ripens after the rainy season is over.

2. The month of Mārgashīrsha, also known as "Agahan"; cf. Glossary.

3. The fruit of the *bel* tree (*Aegle marmelos*) sacred to god Shiva.

4. The water in which rice has been boiled, slightly fermented, is known as *kānjī*.

5. The *nīm* tree (*Azadirachta indica*), a large tree whose leaves are masticated.

6. *khai* : roasted unhusked food-grains, usually paddy.

7. *tāl* (*Borassus flabelliformis*) is the palmyra-tree; its fruit contains a sweet pulp. The sap of the same tree is collected and fermented to make the drink known as *tālī* or *tāḍī* (Engl. "toddy").

डाकेर बचन

बारह मासा*

कार्तिके ओल मार्गे बेल ।
पौषे काञ्जि माघे तेल ।। १ ।।

फाल्गुने आदा चैत्रे तिता ।
बैशाखेते निम नालिता ।। २ ।।

ज्येष्ठे घोल आषाढ़े दहि ।
श्राबने खै भाद्रे ताल ।। ३ ।।

आश्विन शाशा ।
डाक बले एइ बार मासा ।। ४ ।।

*[Nāgarī transcription of the text found in D.C. Sen, History of Bengali Language and Literature, Calcutta 1911, p. 24 note].

II

BADU CHANDĪDĀS : SHRĪKRISHNAKĪRTANA

RĀDHĀ-CHAUMĀSĀ

[old Bengali]

[*Mālavashrīrāga*]

4. The month of Jeṭh is gone, now Āshāḍh is coming,
   dark-blue clouds have spread on the southern sky—
   Yet even now, he has not come back, that cruel son of Nanda ![1]
   so sings Badu Chandīdās, Bāsalī's[2] own servant.

[*Shrīrāga*]

1. In the month of Āshāḍh, clouds are roaring,
   tormented by Madan,[3] my eyes are pouring tears :
   If I but has birds's wings, O Badāyī,[4] I'd fly over there
   where dwells that Kānhaiyā, the Lord of my soul !

How could I endure
those four months of rain ?
My youth in its bloom,
Kānha has made to wither ! [Refrain]

1. The "son of Nanda" is Krishna-Gopāl, the divine Cowherd, Rādhā's Lover. "Kānha" is the Prakrit form of Krishna and "Kānhaiyā" is a diminutive.

2. Bāsalī [devī] is a form of the goddess Kālī, whose cult is particularly important in Orissa. The poem suggests a close link between the poet, Chandīdās, and the goddess Bāsalī. It is believes that the poet was attached to a temple of that goddess, under whose protection he was.

3. Madan, lit. "He who maddens (lovers)" is another name of Kām, the Hindu Eros; see Glossary.

4. "badayi", lit. "grand' mother": it is a respectful form of address to an elderly woman. Actually the *badāyī* of the Bengali folk-song stands as a go-between for lovers.

2. In the month of Shrāvan rain falls in torrents,
lying on my couch, I can't find an instant of sleep :
O Lord, how long shall I be tormented by the flower-arrows of Love?
O Badāyī, make me meet my Kānha just now !

3. In the month of Bhādra, darkness prevails day and night,
peacocks, frogs and water-birds[5] make a hubbub—
If in such a month I cannot see the face of Kānha,
anguish will press on my heart until it breaks !

4. At the end of Āshvin, the rains are over,
gone are the clouds, the Kās bushes burst into flower :
Then, if I am deprived of Kānha, vain is my life !
So sings Badu Chandīdās, Bāsalī's own servant.

5. *ḍāhuka,* literally "those who burn", refer to some celebrated water-birds, such as the Chātak or Papīhā, the Sāras and a few others, whose pathetic cries, especially during the rainy season, are popularly interpreted as desperate calls from a bird—lover to his beloved, see Glossary: *Chātak.*

श्रीकृष्णकीर्त्तन*

राधा-चौमासा

(मालबश्रीरागः)

जेठ मास गेल आसाढ परबेश ।
सामल मेघें छाइल दक्षिण प्रदेश ॥
एभों नाइल निठुर से नान्देर नन्दन ।
गाइल वडु चण्डीदास बासलीगण ॥ ४ ॥

(श्रीरागः)

आसाढ़ मासे तब मेघ गरजए ।
मदन कदने मोर नयन झुरए ॥
पाखी जाती नहों बड़ायि ऊड़ी जाओं तथाँ ।
मोर प्राननाथ काण्हाञिँ बसे यथाँ ॥ १ ॥

के मने बञ्चिबो रे बारिषा चारि मास ।
ए भर योबने काण्ह करिले निरास ॥ ध्रु० ॥

श्राबण मासे घन-घन बरिषे ।
सेजात सुतिआँ एकसरी निन्द ना आइसे ॥
कत ना सहिब रे कुसुमशरजाला ।
हेन काले बड़ायि काण्ह समे कर मेला ॥ २ ॥

भादर माँसे आहोनिशि आन्धकारे ।
शिखि भेक डाहुक करे कोलाहले ॥

*[Nāgarī transcription of the text found in ed. B.R.R. Bidvadvallabha, Bangiya Sahitya Parishad, Calcutta, 7th ed. 1961, p. 155.]

तात ना देखिबोँ यबेँ काण्हाञिँर मुख ।
चिन्तिते चिन्तिते मोर फूट जाइबे बुक ॥ ३ ॥

आशिन मासेर शेषे निविड़े बारिषी ।
मेघ बहिआँ गेलेँ फुटिबेक काशी ॥
तबेँ काण्ह बिणी हैब निफल जीवन ।
गाइल बडु चण्डीदास बासलीगण ॥ ४ ॥

III

MĪRĀBĀĪ : PADĀVALĪ

BĀRAHMĀSĀ

[old Braj-Rājasthānī]

Desharāga

O my Beloved,[1]
grant me the vision of Yourself :
Again and again I call on You,
have pity on me—Ho ! [Refrain]

In the month of Jeṭh, for want of water
the bird is in pain—Ho !

In Āshāḍh, the peacock throws its cry
and the Chatāk-bird too calls the cloud[2]—Ho !

In Shrāvan, the rain falls hard
and my friends play the *Tīj*[3]—Ho !

In Āshvin, the shell enjoys in its heart
the drain-drop of Svāti[4]—Ho !

1. Mīrābāī, the princess-poet of Rājasthān, here sings as a *virahiṇī*, a deserted woman lover pining for her divine Beloved, Lord Krishna, to whom this Bārahmāsā is dedicated; see Glossary: *virahiṇī*.
2. Here the rain-cloud of Ashāḍh symbolizes the divine Beloved, the dark-hued Krishna; see Glossary: *chātak*.
3. The third-day of the light fortnight of Shrāvan, which is a great feast for married women; see Glossary: *Tīj*.
4. The twentieth lunar mansion or asterism: the rain-drop of Svāti is eagerly awaited by the Chātak-bird and also by the shell; see Glossary: *nakshatra*; *Svāti*.

In Kārttik comes the *pūjā* to the god[5]
and You are my God—Ho !

In Agahan, it is getting cold :
quick, come to my help—Ho !

In Paush, there is plenty of white frost :
hasten to my help—Ho !

In Māgh, comes the feast of Basant Panchamī[6]
and they all sing *Phāg* songs[7]—Ho !

In the month of Phālgun, they all play the *Phāg*[8]
and the great trees shed their leaves—Ho !

In the month of Chaitra, Desire sprouts in the heart :
grant me a vision of Yourself—Ho !

In the month of Baisākh, the great trees burst into flowers,
the Koil[9] throws its melodious call—Ho !

Putting crows to flight[10] my days have passed in vain,
in vain did I ask Paṇḍits and astrologers—Ho !

Mīrā, the lonely one, is in deep anguish:
when will You grant her Your vision ?—Ho !

5. The whole month of Kārttik, especially the light *paksh* (fortnight), is sacred to god Vishnu, the most sacred day being the eleventh (*ekādashī*): on that day god Vishnu is supposed to wake up from his four-months sleep. Mīrābāī worships Vishnu under the form of Krishna-Gopāl exclusively; see Glossary: *paksha.*

6. The fifth day (panchamī) in the light fortnight of the month of Māgh (January-February) is a feast heralding the beginning of the season of spring; see Glossary: *Basant.*

7. The *Phāg* (or *phagu*) are songs of the season of Spring, on the erotic theme; cf. Glossary: *Phāg* and *supra* p. 21.

8. "Playing the Phāg" refers to the Holī carnival, which takes place on the last day of the month of Phālgun and the first day of the month of Chaitra; see Glossary : *Phāg,Holī.*

9. About the Koil or Kokil-bird, the Indian cuckoo, see Glossary : *Koil.*

10. In Indian folksongs, the crow may be a messenger sent by the woman in love to her far-away lover; in the same context, it is also serves as an omen: putting crows to fly is resorted to by the virahinī, the direction taken by the crow being taken as an indication of the way from which the beloved may come back.

मीरांबाई की पदावली*

राग देश [बारहमासा]

पिया मोहिं दरसण दीजै, हो।
बेर बेर मैं टेरहुं अहे क्रिपा कीजै, हो॥ टेक॥
जेठ महीने जल विणा पंछी दुख होई, हो।
मोर आसाढ़ाँ कुरलहे, घन चात्रग सोई, हो।
सावण मैं झड़ लागियौ, सखि तीजाँ खेलै, हो।
भादवै नदिया वहै, दूरी जिन मेलै, हो।
सीप स्वाति ही झेलती, आसोजाँ सोई, हो।
देव काती में पूजहे, मेरे तुम होई, हो।
मगसर ठंण बहोती पडै, मोहि वेगि सम्हालो, हो।
पोस महीं पाला घणा, अबहि तुम न्हालो, हो।
महा महीं बसंत पंचमी, फागा सव गावै, हो।
फागुण फागा खेलहैं, वणराइ जुरावै हो।
चैत चित्त में ऊपजी, दरसण तुम दीजै हो।
बैसाख वणराइ फूलवै, कोइल कुरलीजै, हो
काग उडावत दिन गया, बूझूँ पिंडत जौसी, हो।
मीराँ विरहिणि व्याकुली, दरसण कव होसी, हो॥ ११५॥

*[*Mīrabāī kī padāvalī*, ed. P. Chaturvedi, Allahabad, śaka 1884, pada 115, pp. 135-136.]

IV

NĀLHA : BĪSALDEV-RĀS[1]

RĀJIMATĪ-BĀRAHMĀSĀ

[old Rājasthānī-Hindī]

1. He went away, the knight-errant,[2] in the month of Kārttik,
he left his palace, beautiful as a Kailās,
    he left his splendid terrace,[3]
and I, standing on the road, have lost my eyes weeping,
    Hunger and thirst have left me:
Tell me, my friend, how could I get sleep again ?

2. In the month of Agahan, the days grow shorter :
O my friends, he did not send me any message—
    or had lightning fallen on the message ?
Over lofty mountains, through narrow passes,
    he went away to a strange, far-away land
from which no letter comes, to which there is no way.

3. See, my friend, the cold month of Paush has arrived :
the young wife is dying—do not blame her !
    tormented with anguish, my body has turned a skeleton,

1. Though the name of "Bisaldev" does not appear in this *Bārahmāsā*, the poem itself is included in the *Bīsaldev-rās*, a lyrical composition of the *rāso* or *rās* type, on the love and separation of King Bīsaldev and his wife Rājimatī (or Rājal). The earliest manuscript extant of the *Bīsaldev-rās* is dated V.S. 1 (1576 A.D.) and the work's authorship is uncertain. It has been attributed to a Jaina poet called "Narapa or "Nālha" by Agarchand Nahta, a well-known scholar from Rājasthan ("Rājasthānī", January, 1940, p. 22).

2. *ulagānā* : about the interpretation of this word, see p. 34.

3. *caubārā* (*cabūtārā*) refers to a pedestal, a raised platform to sit at ease, or a terrace.

I have no more taste for food, I no longer care to bathe my head,
sunshine and shade are one to me
and my own house to me looks like a burning-ground !

4. In the month of Māgh, so biting is the frost
that all the trees in the forest are burnt to cinders—
I too am burning, and the whole world with me ![3]
Under my bodice, my body is afire :
see the distress of your wife away from her husband
And hasten to come back, spurring your camel !

5. In Phālgun, the trees swing under the gusts of wind,
my soul trembles, hunger and sleep have left me.
The days lengthen, the season changes,
but my foolish husband has not come back to me :
if I survive, it is Youth itself, oh my friend,
which buffets me on all sides and makes me shake in the gale !

6. In the month of Chaitra, women take to the battle-field :[4]
away from her husband, how will the poor girl endure?
she wets her bodice with her tears while all make merry!
How could I play the Holī,[5]
I, the wife of a knight-errant ?
If one just pulled my little finger, the whole arm would go away ![6]

7. In Baisākh, women gather coriander,
And they sprinkle fresh betel-leaves with cool water[7]—
I wish the golden jar of my body was used for the sprinkling !

3. While the frost "burns" the forest, the heroine's body is a prey to the "fire of Virah"; see Glossary : *virah*.

4. *caturangī nārī*, lit. "women are like armies with all the four parts": the women have put on their armour for the coming "love-battles"; so adorned, each one looks more terrible than a whole army in battle-array.

5. Starting of the full-moon of Phālgun, the Holī celebration includes the first day of the month of Chaitra, which is the day on which the mock-battles between men and women take place.

6. So emaciated has her whole body become!

7. The spraying and offering of a fragrant betel-leaf by a woman to her beloved is an invitation to love-making.

But my Lord is a fool who knows nothing of true flavour :
he holds his horse's bridle in hand
and he keeps watch at a king's door !

8. See, my sister-in-law,[8] now the month of Jeṭh has come :
withered is my face and my lips are parched dry,
the days of this months are burning terribly,
the young wife's tender feet cannot touch the ground :
in such a brazier, the young wife is burning
Whislt the Haṁsa-bird has deserted the pond for some unknown place[9].

9. In Āshāḍh, masses of clouds have come back,
water murmur in the rivulets, all the dust is gone—
yet even in this month of Āshāḍh, he did not come back!
Oh my mother ! Clouds gallop like mad elephants,
they come running as if love-crazy !
What is he doing, that knight-errant, in that place over there ?

10. In Shrāvan, rain falls in thin streams,
deprived from her beloved, where will the wife find support?
All her friends play the *Kājalī*,[10]
Over there, the Kameḍī-bird builds his nest,
the Pāpīhā cries : "*Piū, Piū*",[11]
Oh ! Unbearable to me is this month of Shrāvan !

11. In Bhādra, the rain falls hard and thick,
lowlands and highlands, all are under water—
as if the Ocean itself had capsided !

8. *jeṭhāṇī* refers to an older sister-in-law, the husband's elder brother's wife): here *jeṭhāṇī* alliterates with *jeṭha*, the month of Jeṭh.

9. Here the Haṁsa-bird symbolizes the husband and the deserted pond the lonely wife; the unknown, far-away place is the Mānsarovar see Glossary: *Haṁsa*.

10. A song and dance of the rainy season; see Glossary : *Kājalī*.

11. The Pāpīhā is another name for the Chātak-bird. ever pining for the rain-drop of Svāti; cf. Glossary : *chātak*.

Dark are the nights, with flashes of lightning,
the clouds bend down as if to meet the earth—
But my Lord sees nothing: he does not turn back, the fool !

12. In Āshvin, the young lady has prepared the *pūjā* to the horse[12]
She has decorated her house, beautiful as a Kailās,[13]
she has whitewashed the grand terrace,
the gate and the outer wall she has whitewashed too—
then, with a glad heart, she has climbed to her gaükhā:[14]
For now he will come back soon, that foolish husband !

12. The *pūjā* to the horse is performed by Rājputs in the month of Āshvin, and is part of the various rites associated with the Dasserā festival in honour of the great Goddess, who is the protector and principal deity of Rājputs. Before Dasserā, the whole house should be whitewashed and decorated, which is the work of women. The wife is happy in her confidence that her husband will not fail to return in time to join in the celebrations of Dasserā, which is *par excellence*; the feast of the Rājputs; see Glossary: *Dasserā*; *pūjā*.

13. See Glossary : *Kailās*.

14. The *gaukha* or *zarokhā*, a typical feature of Rājput architecture, consists in a broad latticed balcony, usually made of carved sandstone, where the ladies of the house can stand and watch the ceremonies held in front of the palace, without being seen.

राजमती—बारहमासा

चालियउ उलगाणउ कातिग मास ।
छोडीया मंदिर घर कबिलास ।
    छोडीया चउबारा चउषंडी ।
तठइ पंथ सिरि नयण गमाइया रोइ ।
    भूष गई त्रिस ऊचटी ।
कहि न सषीय नींद किसी परिहोइ ॥ भु० ॥ [६७]

मगसिरियइ दिन छोटा जी होइ ।
सषीय संदेसउ न पाठवइ कोइ ।
    संदेसइ ही बज पडयउ ।
ऊँचा हो परवत नीचा घाट ।
    परदेसे परभुइं गयउ ।
तठइ चीरीय न आवइ न चालए बाट ॥ भु० ॥ [६८]

देषि सषी हिव लागउ छइ पोस ।
धण मरतीय को मत दीयउ दोस ।
    दुषि दाधी पंजर हुई ।
धान न भावए तज्या सिरि न्हाण ।
    छाहड़ी धूप न आलिंगइ ।
देषतां मंदिर हुयउ मसांण ॥ भु० ॥ [६९]

माह मास इसीय पड़इ ठंठार ।
दाधा छइ बनषंड कीधा हो छार ।
    आप दहंती जग दह्यउ ।
म्हाकी चोलीय माहि थी दाधउ छइ गात्र ।
    धणीय बिहूणी धण ताकिजह ।
तं तउ उवइगउ रे आविज्यो करह पलाणि ।। भु० ।। [७०]

फागुण फरह् रया कंपिया रूष ।
चितह चमकियउ निसि नींद न भूष ।
    दिन राया रितु पालटी ।
म्हाँकउ मूरष राउ न देषइ आइ ।
    जीवउं तउ जोवन सषी ।
फरहरइ चिहुं दिसि बाजइ छह बाइ ।।भु०।। [७१]

चेत्र मासइ चतुरंगी हे नारि ।
प्रीय बिण जीविजइ किसइ अधारि ।
    कंचूयउ भीजइ जण हसइ ।
म्हे किउं होली हे षेलण जांह ।
    उलगांणइ की गोरडी ।
म्हांकी आंगुली काढ़तां निगलीजइ बांह ।।भु०।। [७२]

बइसाषइ धुर लूणीजइ धान ।
सीला पाणी अरु पाका जी पान ।
    कनक काया घट सींचिजइ ।
म्हाकउ मूरष राउ न जाणए सार ।
    हाय लगामी ताजणउ ।
ऊभउ सेवइ राज दुआरि ।।भु०।। [७३]

देषि जेठाणी हिव लागउ छइ जेठ ।
मुह कुमलाणा नइ सूक गया होठ ।
मास दिहाडउ दारुण तवइ ।
धण कउ हे धरणि न लागए पाउ ।
अनल जलइ धण परजलइ ।
हंस सरोवर छंडि गयउ ठांउ ॥ भु० ॥ [७४]

आसाढ़इ धुरि बाहुड्या मेह ।
खलहल्या षाल नइ बह गई खेह ।
जइ रि आसाढ़ न आवई ।
माता रे मइगल जेउं पग देइ ।
सद मतवाला जेउं ढुलइ ।
तिहि धरि ऊलग काइ करेइ ॥ भु० ॥ [७५]

स्रावण बरसइ छइ छोटीय धार ।
प्रीय विण जीविजइ किसइ अधारि ।
सहु कोइ षेलइ काजली ।
तठइ चिडीय कमेडीय मंढिया आस ।
बाबहियउ प्रीय प्रीय करइ ।
मोनइ अणख लगावइ हो स्रावण मास ॥ भु० ॥ [७६]

भाद्रवइ वरिसइ छइ गुहिर गंभीर ।
जल थल महियल सहु भर्‌या नीर ।
जाणे कि सायर ऊलट्यउ ।
निसि अंधारीय बीज षिवाइ ।
बादल धरती स्यउं मिल्या ।
मूरख राउ न देषइ जी आइ ॥ भु० ॥ [७७]

आसोजइ धण मंडिया आस ।
मंडिया मंदिर घर कबिलास ।
  धउलिया चउबारा चउषंडी ।
सा धण धउलिया पउलि प्रकार ।
  गउष चड़ी हरषी फिरइ ।
जउ घर आविस्यइ मंध भरतार ।। भु० ।।[७८]

(Ed. M. P. Gupta, Allahabad 1953, st. 72-78).

V

MUHAMMAD JĀYĀSĪ :

NĀGAMATĪ-BĀRAHMĀSĀ

[old Avadhī]

1. Āshādh has come, clouds rumble in the sky,
Virah gathers his troops and beats the war-drum :
Gray, blue-black or white, armies of clouds rush up
and the flocks of white cranes in the sky look like floating banners.
On all sides, flashes of lightning glisten like naked swords,
and menacing clouds shower rain-drops hard as arrows.
When the constellation Ārdrā[1] appears, the earth receives the seed—
but to me, a wife away from her husband, who will pay honour?
Bending, the clouds come down and surround me :
O my lord ! Run to my help, I am in the power of Madan[2] !
Frogs, peacocks the koil and the papīhā-birds[2],
all pierce me with their cries—and life ebbs out of my body.

1. Ārdrā, the 11th among the 28 *nakshatras*, "constellations" of the year (see Glossary : *nakshatra*), is the first constellation of the rainy season. There is a pun here on *ārdrā* (written *adrā* in the text), the *nakshatra* which presides to the sowing of the seed in the fields, and *ādara*, "honour". The sense may be : "Who will give me the seed ?" or "Who will honour me ?" by allusion to the fecundation of the wife by her husband's seed at the onset of the rains; see Glossary : *nakshatra*.

2. About these birds whose cries are heard during the rainy season, see Glossary : *Koil*, *Chātak*.

Now the constellation Pushya[3] has come over my head
and I remain without a protector : who will repair our roof ?
Blessed are those women those husbands are at home,
to them belong honour and pride—
But for myself, away from my beloved spouse,
there is no joy of any kind ! [344]

2. In Shrāvan, clouds are pouring down:
all the fields are flooded—but I am drying in the fire of Virah !
The constellation Punarvasu[3] has appeared—but my husband did not see it :
has he lost his mind, this wise husband of mine ?
I weep tears of blood which flow on the ground
running hither and thither like lady-birds.
My friends have hung swings for swinging with their lovers,
green is the land and their wear saffron clothes—[4]
And my heart too swings to and fro,
tossed up and down by Virah's harsh blows !
Mysterious, unknowable, impassable is the road[5]
and I wander round and round as a bewildered Bhambhirī fly[6] !
Farther than the sight can reach, water covers the earth
and the boat of my life, without its Boatman, cannot move !
Between us stand high mountains, fathomless oceans,
endless forests, thorny jungles :
How then could I go and join you, O my Spouse,
neither feet nor wings have I ! [345]

3. Pushya, the 13th *nakshatra*, actually comes after Punarvasu, mentioned in the next stanza.

4. Green and saffron are most auspicious colours, which women wear on their wedding day, as symbols of fecundity. The swinging itself has an erotic connotation.

5. The road leading to the Beloved.

6. The feminine of *bhambhīrā*, a short-lived insect of the rainy season.

3. Now that heavy month of Bhadra has come, hard, unbearable :
how could I bear those dark nights ?
Empty is my house, my husbands stays somewhere else,
my couch to me seems a she-cobra, biting me again and again !
I remain all alone, holding on to one of my bed-props,
eyes wide open, broken-hearted, I die...
The flashes of lightning, the roar of thunder are a torment to me :
Virah, like Death itself, has taken hold of my soul !
Under the constellation Maghā[7], rains falls with violent gales
and my two eyes drip with tears like the angles of the porch-roof !
When the constellation Purvā appears, the earth is flooded,
while I am drying up like the Āk and Javās plants ![8]
Your young wife has dryed up in this month of Bhādra
and you've not come back to revive her, O my Protector !
Ponds and dry land are overflowing,
sky and earth have become one :
The young wife is drowning in the whirlpool of Youth—
O my Beloved, throw her a buoy ! [346]

4. Kunwār[9] has come, everywhere the waters have receded :
now, O my Beloved, return from that foreign land !
Seeing you, my Beloved, my body will revive—
turn your heart towards me, show me your love again !

7. Maghā is the 15th *nakshatra* and Pūrva (or Pūrva-phalgunī) is the 16th : it seems that the 14th *nakshatra*, Āshleshā, which comes after Pushya, has been omitted by the author.

8. The *Āk* and *Javās* plants have the peculiarity of drying up under the rains, just like the *virahiṇī's* body.

9. "Kunwār" is another name of the month of *Āshvin*; see Glossary.

Now the star Agasti[10] has appeared, the clouds of Hasti[11] are rumbling,
saddling their horse, kings rush back to the battlefield,
Chitrā's[12] friend has entered the Fishes's mansion,
crying *Piū-Piū*[13], the Koïl—bird has found its beloved,
The rain-drop of Svāti has fallen into the beak of the Chātak[14],
all the shells in the Ocean are filled with pearls,
Remembering the Mānsarovar lake, the Haṁsas[15] have come back to it,
The Sāras bird is cooing, the Khanjan has reappeared,[16]
Bright is the forest where the Kās bushes are in bloom[17]—
but he, my husband, has not returned, he is lost in a foreign land !

10. The star Agasti (*agastya*) (Canopeus) becomes visible in Northern India at the end of the rainy season, heralding the onset of autumn. When Agasti appears, the monsoon withdraws : this is why the sage Agastya, who gave his name to the constellation, is said to have "swallowed" the ocean.

11. Hasti (or Hasta) "the Elephant", is the 18th *nakshatra*, following Uttara-phalgunī, the 17th, omitted by the author. The elephant-clouds, whose trumpetting is heard at a distance, form the rear of the retiring army of the clouds.

12. Chitrā, the 19th nakshatra, is said to be the friend of the Moon-god Chandramā, since it is under that *nakshatra* that the moon begins again to shine brilliantly in a pure sky.

13. *Piu-piu* is the cry of the Koil-bird, and *piu* means "beloved"; see Glossary : *Koil*.

14. About the Chātak-bird and the rain-drop of Svāti, the 20th *nakshatra*, see Glossary: *Svāti*.

15. About the Haṁsa-birds and the Mānsarovar lake, see Glossary : *haṁsa*.

16. The Sāras is a large water-bird, whose cries during the rainy-season are interpreted as a nostalgic call for its mate—but now it is cooing; the Khanjan is an attractive kind of wagtail, famed for the brilliance and mobility of its eyes.

17. A jungle shrub, which covers itself with pure white blossoms at the end of the rain : those white blossoms are interpreted as the flashing "smile" of the new autumnal season.

The elephant Virah torments my body,
trampling and devouring me—
Hasten, my Beloved, engage the fight,
roar as a tiger and put him to flight ! [347]

5. In Kārttik, the full-moon of autumn rises,
the whole world is refreshed—but I still burn in Virah's fire—
The fourteen digits of the moon spread a cool light,
but to me the whole earth and sky seem afire !
The moon-rays scorch my body and soul and set my couch on fire :
for everyone it is the cooling Moon—but for me it's Rāhū ![18]
If the beloved Husband is not in the house,
it remains plunged in darkness all over.
Now, won't you come home, you, cruel One,
when everybody celebrates the Feast of Lamps ?[19]
All my friends sing and dance the Jhūmar, swinging,[20]
while I am wasting away, separated from my own mate.
Women whose husbands are at home perform the Manorā pūjā[21]
while I endure double torment : that of Virah and that of a co-wife !

My friends celebrate the feast
with songs and dances of Dīvālī—
But how could I play the Dīvālī ?
I keep throwing ashes on my head ! [348]

6. In Agahan, the days grow shorter, longer the nights,
deeper grows my pain—how shall I get over it ?

18. Rāhū is a demon who bites the moon and so causes the eclipse.

19. The great feast of Dīpāvalī or Dīvālī, "the feast of Lamps" in honour of goddess Lakshmī, is celebrated on the *amāvasya* (moonless day) of the month of Kārttik; see Glossary : *Dīvālī*.

20. Jhūmar, a type of song and folk-dance; see Glossary : *jhūmak*.

21. "Manorā" refers to figures drawn upon the house-walls, which are worshipped by women during the Dīvālī festival. Such designs include the representation of a human couple—hence the suggestion of a co-wife, painful to the deserted queen Nāgamatī.

Now the young wife, like the days, looses strength
whilst Virah gets stronger, like the nights !
Feeling the cold, her heart trembles—
only the presence of her beloved could help her get over it.
In each and every house, people have prepared warm clothes—
but my Lord has taken away my beauty and all my finery.
He who deserted me has not returned:
let him but come home and all my finery will be back !
To me the cold has become the fire of Virah which burns my heart:
slowly, slowly burning without a flame, it turned into ashes !
But my beloved does not know the torment I endure
that my life and my youth have turned into ashes !
O you Blackbee, O you Crow,[22]
bring this message to my beloved :
"Your young wife was consumed in the fire of Youth—
t'was the smoke from that fire which turned our wings black !" [349]

7. In Paush, the body trembles, the teeth chatter with cold,
the sun itself feels cold and rushes to warm itself in the South.[23]
As the cold gets more frightful, so Virah increases—
I shiver to death, crying : "O God, take my life !"
O my Spouse, where are you that I may crouch upon your heart ?
Endless is the road to reach you and I hardly know the neighbourhood !
Wrapped in a quilt, I shiver,
as if I had made my couch in the Himalayan snows !

22. The "Bhaṁvār", the Indian blackbee, assumes a particular character in Indian tradition, mostly that of an inconstant lover, yet together with the crow, it also serves as a massenger : both of them are black, the colour of one burnt by the fire of Virah, see Glossary, *bhaṁvār*.

23. In winter, in the Northern hemisphere, the sun seems to withdraw in the direction of the South : here the south is called "the region of Lankā", identified with the ancient capital of Rāvaṇa, the "Lankā" of the *Rāmāyaṇa* Epic; see Glossary : *Lankā*.

The Chakvī-bird is separated from her mate at night—
but at day-break she meets him again :[24]
But I myself, by day and by night,
I am the Kokilā of Virah ![25]
The whole night I remain alone, without even a girl-friend:
how could I, a lonely she-bird, keep alive ?
Virah, like a hawk, hovers in circles over my head
ready to tear me alive : he won't even leave my dead body !

My blood is oozing out, my flesh dissolves itself
and my bones are as dry as empty shells—
Your young wife, like a Sāras-bird,[26] pines to death :
come and alight by her side, folding your wings !
[350]

8. Now Māgh has come and white frost is falling:
Virah, in winter, is frightful as Death !
In vain do I wrap my body in layers and layers of cotton :
the cold increases fourfold—I cannot bear it !
Come, my Protector, be the Sun to warm me up—
without the sun, in Māgh, how could I bear the cold ?
This is the month in which the root of Pleasure blossoms :
as a Blackbee,[27] come and alight on the flower of my youth !
The tears from my eyes are like that early-spring rain[28]
yet the rain burns like fire and its drops like darts,
piercing my clothes,
My tears fall as hard as a hail-storm
and Virah is a strong wind buffeting me !

24. About the Chakvā-Chakvī pair, see Glossary: *chakvā.*

25. In the poet's imagination the black koīl-bird has also been parched by the fire of Virah (cf. *supra* n. 22) : *a fortiori* its female, the kokilā; see Glossary: *koil.*

26. See Glossary : *sāras.*

27. As an inconstant lover, cf. supra n. 22 and Glossary: *bhaṁvār.*

28. *māṁhuṭa* refers to the light clouds which appear in Northern India in January-February, bringing light rain and some hail-storms, and heralding the end of winter.

How then could I adorn myself ? Which precious raiment could I wear ?
My neck cannot bear a necklace : I am thinner than its thread !
O my spouse, away from you, your young wife has wasted away,
her body like a blade of grass fluttering here and there:
Virah has scorched it and now
he wants to blow it away ! [351]

9. In the month of Phālgun, squalls are blowing,
intense is the cold, unbearable !
My body has become like the dry leaves
which the wind of Virah tears off violently !
The great forest-trees and the Dhāk[29] jungle trees loose their leaves
so that their branches are bare of fruit and flowers—
But fresh flower-buds gladden the great trees
whilst the sorrow in my heart increases twofold :
All my friends play the Phāg and dance the Carcarī[30]—
to me it is as if the Holī brazier[31] had been lighted in my very heart !
Were it my beloved's pleasure to see me burning in that fire,
I would endure it without complain:
Day and night, I have no other desire in my heart
O my Spouse, that my ashes may cling to you !

I'll burn this body of mine and reduce it to ashes
and I'll ask the wind to blow them away
So they may fall of that very path
where my spouse's foot will step over them ! [352]

29. The Dhāk tree (*Butea frondosa*) like the Palāsh, with which it is often associated, is a thorny jungle tree.

30. The *phāg* and *carcarī* songs and dances are associated with the Hindu spring festival, known as "Phāg" or "Holī". "Playing the Phāg" is the same as "playing the Holī"; see Glossary : *Holī*; *Phāgu*; *Phālgun*.

31. The main feature of the Holī festival, on the full-moon night of the month of Phālgun, is a huge bonfire lit in the centre of the village or town.

10. In Chaitra, they all sing "Basant" and "Dhamārī"[32]
but to me the whole world seems to lay waste !
Virah-Pancham[33] has let fly his five arrows
and the whole forest is reddened by blood:
All the tender leaves of the trees are bathed in that blood,
the Majīṭh flower is soaked in it and so is the Ṭesu.[34]
Now the mango blossoms have given place to the fruit :
remember your house, come back, O blessed One !
Now the trees are radiant with myriads of shades,
now the bee has come back, remembering the Mālatī flower—
To me all these flowers are like so many thorns
and their sight stinges me like the bite of red-ants !
Heavy are the fruit of Youth on the branch of the orange-tree[35]
and that parrot, Virah, cannot be chased away !

As the homer rushes back to its dove-cot,
so rush home, my beloved,
For your wife has fallen into another's power
and you alone can save her ! [353]

11. Baisākh has come, so great is the heat
that my sandal-scented corselet burns me :
The sun itself, feeling the heat, turns towards the Himālaya[36]
but Virah turns his chariot straight at me !

32. *Basant* (*vasanta*) are songs of spring on the erotic theme; so are the *dhamārī* songs which connote a particular *tāl* or cadence; see Glossary : *Basant*; *Dhamārī*.

33. *Panchama* is the fifth note on the Indian scale, which is associated with the call of the Koil-bird during the mating season, see Glossary. "Pancham" is also one of the names of god Kām or Madan, the Hindu Eros: in spring Virah itself assumes the form of god "Pancham" to torment the deserted lovers; see Glossary : *Kām*.

34. In the season of spring, the dominant colour of the flowering trees is red, the colour of love, which the *virahiṇī* sees as the colour of blood.

35. Allusion to the rounded breasts of the young wife : the devouring parrot is Virah itself.

36. The sun seems to be taking the direction of the North; cp. *supra* st. 7 & n. 23.

In that dreadful fire, I am consumed—O my beloved, overshadow me,
come and put out those live coals :
At your sight, your wife will find relief,
come and turn this inferno into a flower-garden !
I am parched like the grain in the parcher's oven :
parched again and again, I can't escape the hot sand ![37]
The lake of my heart is drying up, little by little it shrinks,
soon it'll crack and burst into pieces:
O my beloved, rush to the help of this, my breaking heart,
be the early rain which smoothes away the cracks of the dry earth !
That lotus which had blossomed in the lake of my soul
withered, lies in the dust—
But in one moment if will revive
if you, my beloved, come back to sprinkle it ![354]

12. In the month of Jeṭh, the world is afire, the Lū[38] is blowing,
rising whirlwinds of dust which parch the hills,
Virah, as a Hanumān, rises with a roar:
he sets my whole body on fire, like another Lankā !
The four winds fan the flames
and from Lankā the fire reaches Palankā ![39]
Consumed in this flame, I turned black as the Kālindī[40] river :
excruciating as a slow fire is the flame of Virah.

37. Allusion to the common process of parching food-grains in India : the parcher throws a handful into a cauldron half-full with burning hot sand over a fire. As the grains dilate or burst, they come up to the surface and the parcher skilfully turns them out with the help of a small broom. But the parched grain, by itself, cannot get out of the cauldron.

38. An oven-hot wind blowing from the Thar desert over the plains of Uttar Pradesh during the summer months (May-June).

39. Allusion to the *Rāmāyaṇa* episode in which the divine monkey Hanumān sets the whole city of Lankā on fire with his blazing tail. "Palankā" is conceived as a very distant land, much beyond Lankā itself. According to the author, the inaccessible mountain on which dwells the object of the hero's quest, princess Padmāvatī, is situated in that mysterious region, and Hanumān himself is its guardian; cf. *Padmāvat* st. 206); see Glossary: *Hanumān*.

40. "Kālindī", "the Black One" is another name of the river Yamunā, known for its dark colour.

The brazier leaps high, the storm comes near,
 but my eyes cannot see it, bound as I am in my sorrow!
Half-burn is my flesh, dried up is my body
 and Virah feeds on it as a ravenous crow :
After eating my flesh, he has started on my very bones—
 do come back now—and he'll fly away at your approach!

Mountains, oceans, clouds, sun or moon,
 there is none that could bear such a blaze :
Says Muhammad, glory be to that holy wife[41]
 who, for the sake of her beloved, endured such torment ! [355]

41. In the poet's eyes, Nāgamatī, the hero's first wife, is a *satī*, a heroic wife determined to follow her husband in death by allowing herself to die on the pyre by his side. But the "fire of Virah" is more cruel than the natural fire, for it is a slow fire, which makes the martyrdom of Virah a more perfect form of martyrdom. For the Sūfī Mahammad Jāyasī, martyrdom, in the form of Virah for the divine Spouse, is the highest spiritual experience. In this, he agrees with the ancient Indian Sūfī Shaikh Farīd and the Sant poet Kabīr:

Do not abuse that Virah
 for Virah is a King :
The body that contains not Virah
 is for ever a burning-ground.
[KABĪR I Sā 3. 16]

पद्मावत

नागमती—बारहमासा

चढ़ा असाढ़ गँगन घन गाजा। साजा विरह दुंद दल वाजा।
धूम स्याम धौरे घन धाए। सेत धुजा वगु पाँति देखाए।
खरग बीज-चमकै चहुँ ओरा। बुंद बान वरिसै घन घोरा।
अद्रा लाग बीज भुइँ लेई। मोहि पिय विनु को आदर देई।
ओनै घटा आई चहुँ फेरी। कंत उवारु मदन हौं घेरी।
दादुर मोर कोकिला पीऊ। करहिं बेझ घट रहै न जीऊ।
पुख नछत्र सिर ऊपर आवा। हौं विनु नाँह मँदिर को छावा।

जिन्ह घर कंता ते सुखी तिन्ह गारौ तिन्ह गर्ब।
कंत पियारा बाहिरें हम सुख भूला सर्ब ।। ३४४ ।।

सावन बरिस मेह अतिवानी। भरनि भरइ हौं विरह झुरानी।
लागु पुनर्बसु पीउ न देखा। भै वाउरि कहँ कंत सरेखा।
रकत क आँसु परे भुइँ टूटी। रेंगि चली जनु बीर वहूटी।
सखिन्ह रचा पिउ संग हिंडोला। हरियर भुइं कुसंभि तन चोला।
हिय हिँडोल जस डोलै मोरा। बिरह झुलावै देइ झँकोरा।
बाट असूझ अथाह गँभीरा। जिउ वाउर भा भवै भँभीरा।
जग जल बूडि जहाँ लगि ताकी। मोर नाव खेवक विनु थाकी।

परबत समुंद्र अगम बिच बन बेहड़ घन ढंख।
किमि करि भेटौं कंत तोहि ना मोहि पाँव न पंख ।।३४५।।

भर भादौं दूभर अति भारी। कैसें भरौं रैनि अँधियारी।
मँदिल सून पिय अनतै वसा। सेज नाग भै धँ धै डसा।

रहौं ग्रकेलि गहें एक पाटी । नैन पसारि मरौं हिय फाटी ।
चमकि बीज घन गरजि तरासा । बिरह काल होइ जीउ गरासा ।
बरिसै मघा झँकोरि झँकोरी । मोर दुइ नैन चुवहिं जसि ग्रोरी ।
पुरबा लाग पुहुमि जल पूरी । ग्राक जवास भई हौं झूरी ।
धनि सूखी भर भाँदौं माहाँ । ग्रबहूँ ग्राइ न सींचसि नाहाँ ।

जल थल भरे ग्रपूरि सब गँगन धरति मिलि एक ।
धनि जोवन ग्रौगाह महँ दे बूड़त पिय टेक ॥ ३४६ ॥

लाग कुग्रार नीर जग घटा । ग्रबहुँ ग्राउ पिउ परभुमि लटा ।
तोहि देखे पिउ पलुहै काया । उतरा चित्त वहुरि करु माया ।
उए ग्रगस्ति हस्ति घन गाजा । तुरै पलानि चढ़े रन राजा ।
चित्रा मित मीर घर ग्रावा । कोकिल पीउ पुकारत पावा ।
स्वाति बुंद चातिक मुख परे । सीप समुंद्र मोति सव भरे ।
सरवर सँवरि हंस चलि ग्राए । सारस कुरुरहिं खँजन देखाए ।
भए विगास काँस वन फूले । कंत न फिरे विदेसहि भूले ।

बिरह हस्ति तन सालै खाइ करै तन चूर ।
बेगि ग्राइ पिय वाजहु गाजहु होइ सदूर ॥ ३४७ ॥

कातिक सरद चंद उजियारी । जग सीतल हौं विरहैं जारी ।
चौदह करा कीन्ह परगासू । जनहुँ जरै सब धरति ग्रकासू ।
तन मन सेज करै ग्रगिडाहू । सब कहँ चाँद भएउ मोहि राहू ।
चहूँ खंड लागै ग्रँधियारा । जौं घर नाहिन कंत पियारा ।
ग्रबहूँ निठुर ग्राव एहिं बारा । परव देवारी होइ संसारा ।
सखि झूमक गावहि ग्रंग मोरी । हौं झूरौं बिछुरी जेहि जोरी ।
जेहि घर पिउ सो मनोरा पूजा । मो कहँ विरह सवति दुख दूजा ।

सखि मानहिं तेवहार सब गाइ देवारी खेलि ।
हौं का खेलौं कंत बिनु तेहिं रही छार सिर मेलि ॥ ३४८ ॥

अगहन देवस घटा निसि बाढ़ी। दूभर दुख सो जाइ किमि काढ़ी।
अब धनि देवस बिरह भा राती। जरै बिरह ज्यों दीपक बाती।
काँपा हिया जानवा सीऊ। तौ पैं जाइ होइ सँग पीऊ।
घर घर चीर रचा सब काहूँ। मोर रूप रँग लै गा नाहूँ।
पलटि न बहुरा गा जो बिछोई। अबहूँ फिरैं फिरैं रँग सोई।
सियरि अगिनि बिरहै हिय जारा। सुलगि सुलगि दगधै भै छारा।
यह दुख दगध न जानै कँतू। जोवन जरम करै भसमंतू।

पिय सौं कहेहु सँदेसरा ऐ भँवरा ऐ काग।
सा धनि बिरहें जरि गई तेहिक धुआँ हम लाग ॥३४९॥

पूस जाड़ थरथर तन काँपा। सुरुज जड़ाइ लंक दिसि तापा।
बिरह बाढ़ि भा दारुन सीऊ। कँपि कँपि मरौं लेहि हरि जीऊ।
कंत कहाँ हौं लागौं हियरें। पंथ अपार सूझ नहिं नियरें।
सौर सुपेती आवै जूड़ी। जानहुँ सेज हिवँचल बूड़ी।
चकई निसि बिछुरैं दिन मिला। हौं निसि बासर बिरह कोकिला।
रैनि अकेलि साथ नहिं सखी। कैसें जिऔं बिछोही पँखी।
बिरह सैचान भँवै तन चाड़ा। जीयत खाइ मुएँ नहिं छाँड़ा।

रकत ढरा माँसू गरा हाड़ भए सब संख।
धनि सारस होइ ररि मुई आइ समेटहु पंख॥ ३५० ॥

लागेउ माँह परै अब पाला। बिरहा काल भएउ जड़काला।
पहल पहल तन रुई जो झाँपै। हहलि हहलि अधिकौ हिय काँपै।
आइ सूर होइ तपु रे नाहाँ। तेहि बिनु जाड़ न छूटै माहाँ।
एहि मास उपजै रस मूलू। तूँ सो भँवर मोर जोबन फूलू।
नैन चुवहिं जस माँहुट नीरू। तेहि जल आगि लाग सर चीरू।
टूटहि बुंद परहि जस ओला। बिरह पवन होई मारैं झोला।
केहिक सिंगार को पहिर पटोरा। गियँ नहिं हार रही होई डोरा।

तुम्ह बिनु कंता धनि हरुइ तन तिनुबर भा डोल।
तेहि पर बिरह जराई कै चरै उड़ावा झोल ॥३५१॥

फागुन पवन भँकोरै वहा। चौगुन सीउ जाइ किमि सहा।
तन जस पियर पात भा मोरा। विरह न रहै पवन होई भोरा।
तरिवर भरै भरै बन ढाँखा। भई अनपत्त फूल फर साखा।
करिन्ह वनाफति कीन्ह हुलासू। मो कहँ भा जग दून उदासू।
फाग करहि सव चाँचरि जोरी। मोहि जिय लाइ दीन्हि जसि होरी।
जौं पै पियहि जरत अस भावा। जरत मरत मोहि रोस न आवा।
रातिहु देवस इहै मन मोरें। लागौं कंत छार जेउँ तोरें।

यह तन जारौं छार कै कहौं कि पवन उड़ाउ।
मकु तेहि मारग होइ परौं कंत धरै जहँ पाउ ।।३५२।।

चैत बसंता होई धमारी। मोहि लेखें संसार उजारी।
पंचम बिरह पंच सर मारै। रकत रोइ सगरौ बन ढारै।
बूड़ि उठे सव तरिवर पाता। भीजि मंजीठ टेसू वन राता।
मौरें आँव फरै अब लागे। अवहुँ संवरि घर आउ सभागे।
सहस भाव फूली वनफती। मधुकर फिरे संवरि मालती।
मो कहँ फूल भए जस काँटे। दिस्टि परत तन लागहिं चाँटे।
भर जोवन एहु नाँरग साखा। सौवा विरह अब जाई न राखा।

धिरिन परेवा आव जस आइ परहु पिय टूटि।
नारि पराएँ हाथ है तुम्ह बिनु पाव न छूटि ।।३५३।।

भा बैसाख तपनि अति लागी। चोला चीर चँदन भौ आगी।
सूरुज जरत हिवंचल ताका। बिरह बजागि सौंहँ रथ हाँका।
जरत वजागिनि होउ पिउ छाँहाँ। आइ बुझाउ अँगारन्ह माँहाँ।
तोहि दरसन होइ सीतल नारी। आइ आगि सों करु फुलवारी।
लागिउँ जरै जरै जस भारू। वहुरि जो भूँजसि तजौं न बारू।
सखर हिया घटत नित जाई। टूक टूक होइ होइ बिहराई।
बिहरत हिया करहु पिय टेका। दिस्टि दवँगरा मेरवहु एका।

कँवल जो बिगसा मानसर छारहि मिलै सुखाइ।
अबहुँ बेलि फिरि पलुहै जौं पिय सींचहु आइ ।।३५४।।

जेठ जरै जग बहै लुआरा । उठै बवंडर धिकै पहारा ।
बिरह गाजि हनिवंत होइ जागा । लंका डाह करै तन लागा ।
चारिहुँ पवन झँकोरै आगी । लंका डाहि पलंका लागी ।
दहि भइ स्याम नदी कालिंदी । बिरह कि आगि कठिन असि मंदी ।
उठै आगि औ आवै आँधी । नैन न सूझ मरौं दुख बाँधी ।
अधजर भई माँसु तन सूखा । लागेऊ बिरह काग होइ भूखा ।
माँसु खाई अब हाँडन्ह लागै । अबहूं आउ आवत सुनि भागै ।
परबत समुँद मेघ ससि दिनअर सहि न सकहिं यह आगि ।
मुहमद सती सराहिऔ जरै जो अस पिय लागि ।।३५५।।

[M. P. Gupta. 2d., 1963, st. 344-355]

VI

BĀRAHMĀSĀ-VARṆANA*

[old Marāṭhī]

1. Chaitra

Verse

How can I pass the moonlit night of Chaitra
in the absence of the noblest of princes ?
So you think, my dear girl friend, that I have enough of merit
to enable me to meet the charming one ?

Song

In the festival of the month of Chaitra, banners are raised,[1]
women worship Gaurī in the sitting posture on the swing,[2]
Southernwood[3] is offered to Bhavānī and Shankara
who are worshipped with great devotion.
But I am deprived from all this, being without my husband.
In fact, I cannot live without him.
Why should the Lord not come to my mansion, oh friend ?

*This translation is the work of Professor S. G. Tulpule, from Poona, India. Professor Tulpule notes that "the poet is anonymous and belongs to the end of the 17th century. It contains the pangs of separation of the wife (?) of king Shahājī of Tanjore (1683-1710) who was then campaigning outside. The poem for each month is divided into two parts called the *Sloka* and the *Daru*, meaning a song."

1. The first day of the light fornight of Chaitra is the Hindu New Year day : on that day banners are raised on the housetops.

2. The swinging takes place of the third day of the light fortnight of Chaitra, called "Gaurī Tīj", in honour of the goddess Gaurī; see also Glossary : *Tīj*.

3. "davanā" (*Artemisia abrotanum*), Engl. Southernwood, is used in the celebration of the feast of the Penates which comes on the full-moon day of Chaitra; the feast itself is also called "davanā". Together with their family deities, the women worship the divine couple Bhavānī-Shankara (god Shiva and his wife Pārvatī).

2. Vaishāka

Verse

How can I bear the heat of Vaishākha
when I am already burning with separation ?
Only the parasol of the merciful love of my husband
will ward off all suffering.

Song

In the month of Vaishākha, Brahmins are worshipped
and given potfuls of sweets and cool water, fans and flowers
and perfumes—[4]
But alas ! I cannot do such service to them
for the memory of my husband haunts me from time to time,
making me restless.
Why should the Lord not come to my mansion, oh friend ?

3. Jyeshṭha

Verse

In the month of Jyeshṭha, I feel very much afflicted
for all my joy is in my husband and he is away.
Supposing I were wicked enough to end my life
his memory will haunt me for ever.

Song

In Jyeshṭha, young girls observe the *vrata* of Vaṭa-Sāvitri[5],
fasting the whole day and giving kumkum and bangles
to married women.
But I do not know of any other vrata than my husband
For no religious observance of any vow vouches his return.
Why should the Lord not come to my mansion, oh friend ?

4. This apparently refers to the feast known as "*gurupushyāmrita*", "nectar and food being offered to the Guru", which falls on the seventh day of the light fortnight of the month of Baishākh (*Vaishākha*).

5. This vrata is performed by girls on the thirteenth day of the light fortnight of the month of Jeth in honour of the *vaṭa* or Banyan-tree (sacred to god Shiva) and of Sāvitrī, a divinized heroin, the most perfect example of wifely devotion : on that day married women, who are supposed to emulate Sāvitrī, are given presents such as kumkum powder and glass bangles which pertain to their own status; see Glossary: *vrata*.

4. Āshāḍha

Verse

The month of Āshāḍha is very painful to me:
Nothing pleases me then—
The only relief would be
to give him a call.

Song

With Āshāḍha begins the Chāturmāsa.[6]
Fasting on the Ekādashī day, they worship Hari and Hara and attain to great merit.
But I need not observe such rigorous vows
for separation from him is by itself a penance.
Why should he not come, oh my friend ?

5. Shrāvana

Verse

In Shrāvana, oh my dear friend,
I have nothing but misery,
isolation is simply unbearable.
It is only the return of the dear one
that can please the lover.

Song

In Shrāvana come the holy mondays dedicated to Lord Shiva[7]
and the Nāg-Panchamī to celebrate snake-worship.[8]
The object is the fulfilment of love
and women, both young and old, indulge in the music of drum-sticks.

6. The Chaturmāsā, the four-months season of the rains, is a period during which many vratas and fastings are practiced : the most important of those is the fasting of the eleventh day of each fortnight during all the four months, beginning with "shayanī eksdāshī" on the eleventh day of the light fortnight of the month of Āshāḍha, the day on which god Vishnu is supposed to fall asleep, and ending on the eleventh of the light fortnight of Kārttik.

7. All the Mondays (Moon-days) of the month of Shrāvan are dedicated to Shiva, the Lord of the moon.

On the full-moon day in this month
are offered sacred strings to gods and Brahmins,[9]
and on the eight is celebrated the festival of sweets.[10]
But even the *Harikathā*[11] causes me pain
for the feeling of separation is ever there.
Why should my Lord not come, oh my friend ?

6. Bhādra

Verse

In Bhādrapada, Vishnu is fast asleep[12]
so they pray the moon

8. "Nāg-panchamī," celebrated on the fifth day (*panchamī*) of the light fortnight of Shrāvan in honour of the nāgas, the divine cobras, is a very popular feast. Women worship and feed the cobras, both living ones and charcoal representations drawn on the walls, with offerings of milk and flowers. There are also dances in honour of the divine snakes.

9. The full-moon day of the month of Shrāvana, "Shravanī-pūrnimā," is an important festival, also known as "Raksha-bandhan". On this day, the twice-born, especially the Brahmins, change their sacred thread (made of three strings) and receive presents. On the same day, sisters tie decorated string bracelets called "rākhī" to their brothers, wrist, as a kind of talisman, and the brothers give them a present in exchange. People living on or near the West coast throw coconuts into the sea, so that the feast is known in Maharashtra as "Naralī-pūrnimā", the "coconut-full-moon."

10. The "festival of sweets" alludes to "Krishna-jayanti", the celebration of Krishna's birthday on the eighth day of the dark fortnight the month of Shrāvan (in other parts of India, of the month of Bhādra). The Vaishnava temples are brilliantly decorated and illuminated and women prepare a number of sweetdishes to be offered to the baby Krishna at night and taken home the next day.

11. The festival of the birth of Krishna includes a number of readings from the Vaishnava Purānas, done by Pandits with appropriate commentories : this is *Harikathā* proper. But devotional singing (*kīrtan*, *bhajan*) of hymns related to the glorious deeds of Krishna are performed everywhere and are well-attended, especially by women. Many of those Krishnaite hymns are composed on the theme of the pangs of separation (*viraha*) endured by the cowherdesses of Braj, the Gopīs—hence the enhancing of suffering for all the women separated from their beloved, such as the wife of Lord Shāhājī.

12. About the sleep of god Vishnu duiing the four months of the rainy season, cf. *supra* n. 6.

Keeping silence
and observing the expiatory Chāndrāyana *vrata.*[13]

Song

In Bhādrapada, in honour of Haritālikā, Protector of the family,[14]
women observe a rigorous vow,
fasting and observing silence.
The town people worship Bhavānī and Shankara,
keeping watch during the night.
On the fourth day, singing and playing instruments,
all the people worship Ganesha, with great devotion.[15]
Had he be at home,
my husband would have done it.
But, alas ! he is away and without him,
I cannot perform the worship,
Why should my Lord not come
O my friend ?

7. Āshvina

Verse

How I wish, oh my friend,
that my dear one should return home
for the festival in the month of Āshvina !
But I really do not know what he wills
and that makes me uneasy.

13. The Chāndrāyana *vrata* is an expiatory fast, recommended during the rainy season. The fast follows the waning and waxing of the moon: from the full-moon day (*pūrnimā*) onwards, the intake of food is decreased by one morsel till the moonless day (*amāvasya*); then it is increased by one morsel till the next full-moon day.

14. The Haritālikā vrata is a 24 hours fast which precedes the "Haritālikā Tīj" also known as "Kājalī Tīj"; see Glossary, *Tīj Kājalī*. It is exclusively a women's festival, whose purpose is said to secure marital, i.e. unwidowed, happiness). The name "Haritālikā' apparently refers to the ancient Mother-goddess Harīti of Harīta, invoked as a protector of children.

15. The Ganesha or Ganapati festival occurs on the fourth day (*caturthī*) of the light fortnight of Bhādrapada. The festival is specially popular in Maharashtra.

Song

In Āshvina is the festival of the Nine Nights[16],
when the Goddess is worshipped for nine days
with great rejoicing.[17]
On the next day, the horses, the elephants and the weapons
are worshipped
with sacrificial rites.[18]
On that day, the "crossing of the boundary" is performed
and the worship of the Shamī tree,[19]
leaves of which are exchanged as gold coins.[20]

16, The festival of Navarātra, the the "nine nights" (and days) in honour of the warlike goddess Durgā, occurs twice a year: in spring, in the month of Chaitra, and in autumn, in the month of Āshvina; the latter is of much greater importance in Northern India and also in Maharashtra, especially for the warlike castes; it ends on the tenth day, which is the Dasserā festival; see Glossary, *Dasserā*.

17. During the Navarātra, the goddess is worshipped every night under a different name from the first till the eighth day of the light fortnight of Āshvina. Simultaneously, a famous poem in praise of the goddess, known as the *Devī-mahātmyam,* in sanskrit, is chanted. On the night of the eighth day, a blood-sacrifice is performed and the blood of a buffalo or a goat is offered to the goddess. Curiously, this very important rite is not mentioned here : it may be attributed to the repugnance of the author, who may have been Vaishnava : the Vaishnavas never approved of that rite and when they performed it, they did it symbolically.

18. On the day following the blood sacrifice to the goddess, kings and warriors worship their vehicles (horses and elephants) and their weapons. The king is accompanied by his own "purohit" who perform Vedic rites here mentioned as *homa-havana.*

19. On the same day "the king"—or any local chief or important personality—leads a men's procession to the village boundary. They symbolically perform the "crossing of the boundary" (*śīmollanghana)* and worship the Shamī tree which ought to be found at that particular spot. This rite is a pre-condition to the beginning of any military expedition. The Shamī tree (*Mimosa suma*) is considered as a Mother-goddess, of the nature of fire or "Mother of fire".

20. On that day, leaves of the Shamī tree are eagerly collected by the people and exchanged between them as if they were gold coins. In popular belief gold is "solidified fire".

The fourteenth day is the festival of Lights,[21]
lasting for full four days,
when men and women wave lights round the face of their spouses.
But all that is denied to me,
and I really do not know when favourable times will greet me :
Why should my Lord not come to my house, oh friend ?

8. Kārttika

Verse

The month of Kārttika has arrived, oh friend,
and still my husband is not even reckoning me.
What wrong have I done
that my Shāhārāj should treat me like this ?

Song

In Kārttika, people perform the Ekādashī and the Dvādashī vratas[22]
and worshipping the Tulasī[23] and the Āvalā plants,

21. On the last day of the dark fortnight of Āshvina, the "Feast of lamps", Dīpāvalī or Dīvālī, is celebrated; see Glossary : *Divālī.* Actually the festival is spread over four days : the two last days of the dark fortnight of Āshvin, respectively called "Choti Dīvālī" and "Dīvālī" proper or "Lakshmī-Kuber-pūjā", and the first two days of the light fortnight of Kārttika : on the first "Govardhan-pūjā", a pastoral feast in honour of the Govardhan hill and the cattle; on the secund "Bhāu-bīj", which is a feast in honour of the Yamunā river and also a feast of all "brothers", who, on that day, are entertained by their sisters.

22. The ekādashī of the light fortnight of Kārttika is specially important to all Vaishnavas as the day of the "awakening" of god Vishnu (cf. *supra* n. 6) and so it is spread over two days and includes the secund day, the dvādashī.

23. After the Kārttika Ekādashī festival comes the Tulasī-vivāha festival i.e. the celebration of the annual "marriage" or god Vishnu, normally under the form of the shaligrām stone, with the goddess Tulasī (the Tulasī plant, *Ocymum sanctum*). The Tulasī-vivāha ceremony is performed in Vaishnava homes between the ekādashī and the pūrṇimā of Kārttika.

they enjoy picnics with Hari.[24]
I will also celebrate the festival in all faith
but only when the Lord of my life returns in resounding glory.
That is my vow. Why should he not come to me then ?

9. Mārgashīrsha

Verse

How I look in the direction of my husband in that month of Mārgashirsha
and how miserable I feel !
He has no mercy for me
and still I crave for his arrival.

Song

The month of Mārgashirsha is very dear to Hari.[25]
It is called Dhanurmāsa, with early morning worship.[26]
A variety of foods are first offered to the deity
and then partaken along with Brahmins.
Now comes the festival of Campāshashthī,
when Mārtāṇḍa-Bhairava is worshipped with great devotion.[27]
But tell me, my friend, what I should do
when the Lord of my life is still away from me ?
Why should he not come to my house, oh friend ?

24. The Āvalā or Āmalaka tree (*Emblic myrobolam*) yields a fruit which is credited with rejuvenating power. During the month of Kārttika, people enjoy picnics under the Āvalā trees. The feast called "Āvalī-bhojana" on the fourteenth day of the light fortnight of Karttik, is the concluding day of the festival which is very popular in Maharashtra. It is also the day on which the "Gopāla-kālā" festival is held in Pandharpur among Vaishnavas, in memory of a picnic held by Krishna-Gopāl with his companions from Braj.

25. So says the *Bhagavad-gitā*, 35 : "among the months I am Mārgashīrṣha".

26. "Dhanurmāsa" corresponds to the period in which the sun is in the Zodiac singh "Dhanu" (Sagittarius), a period which coincides roughly with the month of Mārgashīrsha (or Agahan). Food offering are made in the morning, preferably before sunrise.

27. The feast of the goddess Champāshashtī—which falls on the sixth day of the light fortnight of Mārgashīrsha is said to coincide with the "rising" or arising" of god Mārtaṇḍa-Bhairava, who is popularly identified with god Shiva's son, Skanda. "Mārtaṇḍa" (lit. "the sun") is also a name assumed by Khandobā, the form of Skanda most popular in Maharashtra.

10. Pausha

Verse

The month of Pausha has arrived,
but tell me when my husband will ?
How can I sustain my life
in separation from him ?

Song

Pausha has arrived, and along with it
the festival of Sankrānti which all are celebrating.[28]
It is an auspicious time
when youg married girls are busy
taking sesame-bath and giving away lamps and Badarī fruits
and turmeric and Kumkum.
I too would have done these rites of married women
only my husband should have been here.
How can I make offerings in his absence ?
Why should he not come to my mansion, oh my dear friend?

11. Māgha

Verse

It is now many days since my husband is away,
how long should I suffer the pangs of separation ?
In fact how can I live without him ?

Song

The Shivarātrī in the month of Māgha is a vow
practised by all with regularity.[29]
Fasting, worshipping Shiva and night-waking,
it is celebrated. On tne next day

28. The festival called "Makara Sankrantī" marks the entrance of the sun into the "makara" zodiac sign, corresponding to the Capricorn. Being a solar feast, it has no fixed place in the lunar calendar, but it occurs within the month of Paush. On that day, the use of sesame-seed (*til*) or sesame. oil is recommanded, and eatables are made with it.

29. The "Shivarātrī" or "Mahāshivarātrī", "the great Night of Shiva" is the major Shaiva festival in the Hindu calendar. The vrata and the festival are widely observed, but it is of special importance to Shaiva ascetics. It occurs on the thirteenth day of the dark fornight of the month of Māgh.

People feed the Brahmins—then they break their fast.
But there is no breaking of the fast for my eyes,
for I feel restless without my husband.
It is now many, many days since we met
and I have become thirsty for him.
Why should he not come to me, oh my friend ?

12. Phālguna

Verse

O my dear friend, my Prince has come back
for the festival of Phālgun !
I am very happy
to see the merciful one again.

Song

The month of Phālgun has come,
and the spring festival has begun.
Sprinkling coloured powder and perfumed water on each other,
and singing and dancing,
people are making merry.[30]
The Lord of my life is back home
and I am contented.
All my sorrow has gone away
and I am happy in the re-union.

30. About the Phālgun festival, cf. V st. 9 & fn. —30, 31; see also Glossary : *Phāg*; *Holī*.

।। बरामासवर्णन ।।

(बनाम)

चैत्रमास श्लोकः—

कसी चांदणी रात्री गे चैत्रमासीं
क्रमु योग नसतां नृपालोत्तमासीं
कसा काय माझा असे पुण्यरासी
सये योग होईलसा सुंदरासी ।। १ ।।

दरु

चत्रमासीं सण करिती गुढचा उमारिती ।
संतोषें घरोघरींही दोळा
बैसऊनी गौरी पूजिती नारी ।
दबना वो भवानी शंकरा अर्पिती
भक्तिने पूजा शक्तिने करिती ।
सये मज पतीवीण काहीहीं घडेना
मना आवडेना रमणा वेगळे वो ।। १ ।।
सखीये कां वो शाहभूपती मंदिराप्रति ।

वशाखमास श्लोकः—

वियोगा तपें तप्त वैशाखमासी
कसे काय सोसील उष्णांगमासी ।
पतीचे दया छत्र सौंरक्षणासी
जरी होय तें सर्व संतापनासी ।। २ ।।

दरु

वैशाखमांसी अखथीज पृजुनी द्विज ।
हेती घटभरूनी पकान्ने सहित
सफल जलशीतळ छत्र पदुका व्यजन
सुगंध सुमन चंदन देती सज्जन
मज काहीं न घड़े पतीचे स्मरण ।
घड़ेषडे होते मन पीडे ।
निष डोळां न पडे ।। २ ।।
सखीये कां वो शाह्भूपती मंदिराप्रति ।

जेष्ठमास श्लोकः—

सबे जेष्ठमासी भला कष्ट होती
असे तुष्टी पुष्टी पतीचेच हाती
जरी नष्ट होऊन गे दुष्ट भावें
नये नष्ट से प्राण जाण स्वभावे ।। ३ ।।

दरु

जेष्टमांसी वङ् सावित्री व्रत ।
युवती नेमाने करिती उपवास
एकवार प्रायाचित पूजा निश्रित ।
करुनिया वो देती सौभाग्य वाणें
सुवासिणोस सोळाजणीस ।
मी दो कांही वो नेणे पति वांचुनी व्रत दो
वसा नसे भरवसा पति वेगी याषास ।। ३ ।।
सखीये कां वो शाहभूपती मंदिराप्रति ।

आषाढ़मास श्लोकः—

आषाढमासी सखी होय पीडा
न गोड बाटे मत्र गेह बाडा

नसे तया चाड मुळाच वाडा
कुडा मनीसा पति भान काढा ॥ ४ ॥

दरु

चातुर्मास ग्रारंभ संभ्रम ब्रतोपक्रम ।
ग्राषाढमासी करिती एकादशी
निराहार देव हरिहरा (स) ।
पूजूनिया धरिता शाकादिकें
व्रत द्वीदळ तेणं निस्तुळ ।
पुण्य पावती ज़न मन सर्वदा
व्रत उपवास पती सइवास नसतां घडतसे ॥ ४ ॥
सखीये कां वो शाहभूपती मंदिराप्रती ।

श्रावणमास श्लोकः—

सबे श्रावणांत प्रियाचा वियोगे
सदा सौख्य नाहि भला दुःख योगें
कां येइल प्राणनाथ स्त्रियाला
मुदाधिक्य होतें तसेच प्रियाला ॥ ५ ॥

दरु

श्रावण सोमवार व्रत ईश्वर ।
प्रीतीकारणे रीती पंचमीस
नागपूजन युवतीजन ।
ग्रानंदे नायनासी टिपरी
घाळिती ग्रबळा मिळोनी बाळा ।
पीवंती पुनवेसी देव द्विजास वो
ग्रर्पिती बसे तर्पिती ।
मृष्टान्ने करुनिया ग्रष्टमीस
उत्सव करिती मव ।
पीडित हरिकथा मज सखी

पति वियोग व्यथा असे सर्वदा
कधी येईल सांगे ॥ ५ ॥
सखीये कां वो शाहभूपती मंदिराप्रती ।

भाद्रपदमास श्लोकः—

सये भाद्रमासांत गे गाढ निद्रा
उपेंद्रास लागे तथा मौनमुद्रा ।
करिताती चंद्रास वारुण्य सांद्रा
पडे विस्मृती माजि तैसी नरेंद्रा ॥ ६ ॥

दरु

भाद्रपदी कुळपाळिका हरितालिका ।
व्रत करिती नेमें निराहार
उपवास करूनि मौन धरूनि ।
भवानी शंकराचे पूजन
करूनि नागर रात्री जागर ।
गीतबाद्य सहित चौबीस
गणेश पूजन भक्तिने जन ।
करीती सये पाहे पती जरी सये
गांवीं असतां तरी पुसतां ।
माझा व्रत वो वसनां वो नेणे
पतिबांचुन व्रत पूजन कैसे करूं वो काय ॥ ६ ॥
सखीये कां वो शाहभूपती मंदिराप्रती ।

आश्वीनमास श्लोकः—

सबे आश्वीनांतील गे उत्सवासी
प्रिये यावें असेच वाटे जीवासी
कसे काय येईल त्याचे मनासी
मला तेच गे होतसे साधनासी ॥ ७ ॥

दरु

आश्वीनांत नवरात्र वो सये सर्वत्र ।
देवी पूजन जप उत्सव करूनी
नवु दीवस सये नवमीस ।
होम हवन करूनी अश्वगज
शस्त्र पूजीती बहु साजती ।
वस्त्र भूषण धरुनी दसमीस
सीमोलंघन शमी पूजन करूनी ।
गीतवाद्यसहित वो घारास आणून
सोने मानुन देताती रमणीस ।
दीपोत्सव चतुर्दसीस
चारीदिवस बहु उत्सव करिती ।
वोवाळिती नरनारी वो
प्रीतिभरी वो असोनी रमणाची ।
मजवरीं नयेसा झाला वो
माझा काळ वो कधी ये अनुकूळा ॥ ७ ॥
सखीये कां वोभ शाहपती मंदिराप्रति ।

कार्तिकमास श्लोकः—

सबे मास आला असे कार्तीकाचा
समाचार नेघे पति गे फुकाचा
असा काय अन्याय देखोनी माझा
नयें मी करुं काय गे शाहाराजा ॥ ८ ॥

दरु

कार्तिकमासी एकादसी
तैसी द्वादसीव्रत नेमाने करूनी ।
तुळसी आवळी पूजन
वनभोजन करिती हरीचा वो ।

प्रबोधोत्सव बहु आदरें
सये गजरें कधी येईल प्राणपति ।
माझा मी करीन उत्सव
तेच दिवसी वो ऐसा माझा नवस ।। ८ ।।
सखीये कां वो शाहभूपती मंदिराप्रति ।

मार्गशीर्षमास श्लोकः—

कसा मार्ग मासांत गे मार्ग पाहो
पतीचा वियोगें किती दुःख पाहो
कृपा स्वास नाही व पाही मला वो
नृपाचाच याया उपाया जपावे ।। ९ ।।

दरु

मार्गशीर्षमास हरीकथा
अति प्रीतीचा ह्मणोनी ।
धनुर्मासी प्रातःकाळी पूजन
न्यारु चित्रान्ने निवेदन करूनी ।
ब्राह्मणसहित भोजन
करिती जन चंपासष्टीचा सण ।
मार्तांडभैरव भक्तीने
निजभक्तीने पूजती सबे ।
माझा प्राणपति अपूण न ये
करू मी काय ते वो मज तुं सांगे ।। ९ ।।
सखीये कां वो शाहभूपति मंदिराप्रति ।

पौषमास श्लोकः—

सबे मास आला असे पौष गेहा
कधी सांग येईल भर्त्तार गेहा
वियोगे तयाचा कसे प्राण पाहा
घरावें सखे म्या तथा या स्वदेहा ।। १० ।।

दरु

पौषमास आला दो जाण
संक्रांती जाण करिती सर्व जण ।
पूर्वकाळीं तीळस्नान वो
दीपदान वो देती वधूजन ।
वाणें सुगडांची घालुनीया तीळ
बदरीफळ परस्परें इळदी कुंकुम ।
दे(ऊ)नी भरिती बोंटी
अतिप्रीति असतांजरि गांवि पति ।
माझा करितें मीहीं व्रत
दान सांप्रत ऐसे कैंसे कराये ।। १० ।।
सखीये कां वो शाहभूपती मंदिराप्रति ।

माघमास श्लोकः—

बहुदीस झाले कसे म्या करावे
पतिचा वियोगें किती म्या झुरावे
नृपावांचुनी देह कैसे धरावे
सये स्वास गे आपनाही परावे । ११ ।।

दरु

माघमासी शिवरात्री वो
व्रत सर्वत्र करिती नियमाने ।
उपवास निराहार शंकर पूजा
उपहार तैसा रात्री जागर
करूनीया ब्राश्रण तर्पण
सये पारणें करिती सैये ।
माझा डोल्याचे पारणे फिटेना
घर बाटेना पतिवांचुनि कांही ।
गेले सैये बहुदिवस
गजला आस लागलीसे वो फार ।। ११ ।।

सखीये कां वो शाहभूपती मंदिराप्रती ।

फाल्गुणमास श्लोकः—

सये फाल्गुणांतील गे उत्सवाला
अति प्रीतीने भूप मांवासी वाला
मला ताजगी घोर संतोष झाला
कृपाळास देखोनीया गे नृपाळा ।। १२ ।।

दरु

आला वो फाल्गुण मास हा
उप्सव महा करिती वशंताचा ।
खेळती अबीर गुलाल
सुमनजळ सिंपती एकमेकावरी ।
नारीनर बहु संतोषे
गानविलासे करिती सये ।
माझा प्राणपति आला गांवास
झाला जीवास बहुतहीं संतोषें ।
गेले माझें सफल दुःख
झालेसे सुख पतीचा वो संयोगे ।। १२ ।।

इति बारामास वर्णन संपूर्ण ।

VII

VINAYACANDRA SURĪ : NEMINĀTHA-CHATUSPADIKĀ

RĀJAL—BĀRAHMĀSĀ [old Gujarātī]

1. Having invoked the blessed Lord [Neminātha]
of dark-blue hue, full of grace and beauty,
Listen to the dialogue of Rājal with her girl-friend
as it is related in the form of a Bārahmāsā.
For the love of prince Nemi, at Girnār,
The princess Rājal turned a Siddhī ![1] [Refrain]

2. In the month of Shrāvan, the clouds roar loudly
and my body is burnt in the fire of Separation
Flashes of lightning, to me, are like devouring monsters:
O my friend, how shall I survive without Nemi ?

3. "On my Lady, says her girl-friend, do not grieve !
let all the wicked's plans be frustrated :
Nemi is gone—and then what ?
there are enough husbands to be found !

4. But Rājal makes this reply :
There is no royal spouse equal to Nemi !
All the stars appear to shine on the sky-vault
but once the sun rises, they all fade away.

1. About the legend of the renunciation of Neminãth and Rājal, cf. *supra*, Part I, pp. 21-22. *Siddhī* is the feminine of *Siddha* "a perfect ascetic", one who has achieved final liberation.

5. In the month of Bhādra, all the ponds brim full of water
   at this sight, Rājal weeps piteously :
   "How could you abandon me, alone, without protector,
   you, the Ocean of compassion ?"

6. Her friend tells her : "O Rājal ! Do not weep !
   That cruel Nemi won't ever be yours :
   If one waters a noble tree, it grows green
   but a hard, rocky hill just gets harder !"

7. "You are right, O my friend ! Even if a rock could be softened,
   my dark-hued spouse would not be :
   Under pouring rain, the pond overflows
   but a whole array of clouds will just make the sea dance.[2]

8. In the month of Āshvin, it is a stream of tears
   that flows from Rājal's eyes, away from Neminath :
   "Moon rays and sandal-paste, cool as snow, burn me :
   without the presence of my spouse, all is torment to me !"

9. "O my friend ! Stop pining for that Nemi !
   Don't let yourself waste away for his sake—
   He who, after showing love for you,
   has deserted you, scorning a love of eight births."[3]

10. "Nemi is merciful, O my friend ! He is guiltless :
    it was all the fault of Ugrasen[4] :
    It was he who had locked all those animals in the yard
    and so raised a quarrel with my Beloved."

2. Rājal means to say that her beloved Nemi is "harder"—i.e. firmer—than any rock or mountain; his power and grace are as vast as the sea, to which no pond can be compared.

4. Ugrasen is the king, father of the princess Rājal : the latter chooses to throw the blame for the rupture on her royal father.

3. A perfect, ideal wife, a true *satī* wishes for and obtains from Destiny to follow her husband from birth to birth, i.e. to be his wife in eight successive lives : "a love of eight births" is a proverbial expression.

11. Comes the month of Kārtik, the constellation Kṛttik
appears :
Rājmatī's body is wasting away, her soul is in turmoil:
Day and night, she laments and cries :
"Come back, come back ! Have pity, have pity, O my
spouse !"

12. "O my friend, give up the hope to see Nemi again
that coward has deserted his own house :
Who, but a coward, would desert such a loving wife
to run away to Girnār ?"

13. "How dare you call a coward the glorious Nemi,
him who on the battlefield has defeated so many kings?
So long as a breath remains in this body of mine
I won't give up the the hope of being re-united to
Nemi !"

14. In the month of Mārgashīrsha, the young girl is still waiting
and she speaks those words that fair one with the
large eyes:
"For that one who will bring Prince Nemi back to me
I'll do anything, any time !"

15. "Don't be so obstinate, O my friend !
What can you expect from that Nemi, O dear ?
Whoever has been forcibly seated on the macān
can't be counted upon to frighten away the birds !"[5]

16. "O my friend, during eight lives past I have been serving
Nemi :
how then could I not be devoted to him alone ?
Even if my Lord scorned me
I would ever remained attached to his name."

5. The *macān* (Skt *mañca*) is a light platform set up a tree which serves as a post of observation for a man in charge of minding the ready crop and frightening away the birds with repeated shouts, a tedious occupation. The proverb suggests that, it Nemi is brought back to Rājal by force, he will prove of no use as a lover.

17. In the month of Paush, give up your anger, O my Master!
Save me, save me from Madan's blows !
In the cold, the nights seem never to end—
all sorrows and pains fall upon me all at once !

18. "O you, naive girl ! You keep crying "Nemi, Nemi !"
unaware that your own youth is passing away :
This world is full of wonderful men,
do take another husband !"

19. "You yourself, my friend, are a foolish woman, quite a stupid one !
When I have Prince Nemi as a spouse
How could I ever care for another man ?
Does one dismount an elephant to ride a donkey ?"

20. In the month of Māgh, cold increases,
the noble lady cries : "O Beloved, take me to your side !"
Far from you, O my Lord, I am hard bitten by the cold
and Māra keeps dealing me blow after blow !"[6]

21. "O my friend, says her girl-friend, you're wasting your tears !
Can one subdue an elephant by catching its ear ?
Have you not yet understood, my dear lady,
that your Nemi has left you to run after a beautiful Siddhī ?"

22. "My Spouse has his dwelling in my heart :
how could I believe your words, O cruel girl ?
And if he had gone after a Siddhī, what of that ?
By his side I would ever be Ugrasen's daughter !"[7]

6. In Buddhist and Jaina literature, the god of love, Kāma or Madana is often called Māra "he who strikes down" or "kills"; see Glossary : *Kām.*

7. Even if Nemi had an affair with a woman-ascetic, she, the Princess Rājal, king Ugrasen's daughter, would ever remain the wedded wife of Prince Nemi.

23. In the month of Phālgun, gusts of wind make the leaves fall:
as if the trees themselves were weeping over Rājal's sorrow !
Trembling all over, that Daughter-of-the Earth[8] cries out :
"Why did I not die in my mother's womb ?"

24. "Now, my friend, listen to my word :
there are many husbands just as good as Nemi—
And then, my friend, when one cannot get "modak" sweets
and one is hungry, simple pancakes are appealing !"

25. "If there were a horseman faster than thought,
he would not yet be equal to Nemi !
O my friend, none shall I wed but that dark-hued hero :
would the chātak-bird drink anything but the cloud drop ?"

26. In the month of Chaitra, trees are in bloom in the forest,
each grove resounds with the cry of the Koil-bird :[10]
God Kām has set his five arrows on his bow[11]
and he has pierced the heart of the lady Rājal.

27. "See, my friend, the wild merry-making of Spring—
but she only can play "Basant"[12] whose husband is at home :
It is with him that she can engage in ever-new love plays
and drink deep of the pleasures of life and youth !"

8. The earth which supports all living beings, is a symbol of "firmness": the princess Rājal too, as a parangon of firmness, is called "daughter-of-the earth," which makes an antithesis with the adjective *vihangalā* "agitated, trembling".

9. About the Chātak-bird, see Glossary : *chātak*; here the rain-cloud symbolises the dark-hued Nemi and the Chātak-bird the virahinī Rājal.

10. See Glossary : *koil.*

11. See Glossary : *Kām.*

12. See Glossary : *Basant*; "playing Basant" is enjoying the season of spring with appropriate songs, dance and love-play.

28. "Listen, O my friend ! Nemi had taken me me for his wife,
never did he break his word—
If Nemi is not true to his word
then I'll give up both youth and life !"

29. In Baisākh, tall forest-trees are covered with flowers,
Madan's friend, the sweet-scented Malaya breeze[13], is blowing—
"Burst, O my heart" cries Rājal—for Basant is within
and she sees her Spouse within her own heart.

30. To make her forget her sorrow, her friend tells her :
"Listen to the humming of the blackbee :[14]
Youth lasts but a few days—
meanwhile let us eat, drink and make merry !"

31. The girl Rājal looks with envy on the other women :
"Blessed are they, who enjoy their husband's love—
Unfortunate, wretched indeed are those
who could not obtain the vision of their Beloved !"

32. In the month of Jeṭh, Separation burns like another sun[15],
the river-streams are dryed up under that unbearable torment—
Seeing the Champak-buds in bloom,[16]
Rājal has fainted, in an agony of love.

13. The sweet-scented Malaya breeze (see Glossary : *Malaya*) stands as an objective ally of the god of Love.

14. Bhamvār, the blackbee which hovers from flower to flowe is a great lover; see Glossary : *Bhaṁvār*.

15. Virah, the pain of separation, parches the heroin's soul like the fierce sun of the month of Jeṭh, the hottest month of the year : it is the some fire of Virah which dries up the stream.

16. The fragrant blossoms of the Champak-tree are another lure for the Bhaṁvār.

33. "Come quick, O my friends ! The princess has fainted,
she has fallen down, stiff as a sword !"
The sweet scent of sandal has revived her
and her friends comfort her with loving words.

34. Says the noble lady : "I have grown disgusted with this world,
waiting for you so long, O you the noblest of the Yādavas !
Now, I my Lord, be true to your word
and take me to Girnār !"

35. In the month of Āshāḍh, Rājal has taken heart,
to the roar of thunder and lightning she pays no heed—
She, Ugrasen's daughter, utters these words :
"Let me practice Dharma[17], let me serve at my Husband's feet.

36. Rājal meets her friend, who reproaches her, saying :
"Can one chew black pepper as if it were chickpea ?
Hold your tongue, my dear, and don't talk such nonsense :
Hard indeed is the way of asceticism—and you are so delicate !"

37. "For eight lives I enjoyed my husband's company,
O my friend, now my soul no longer craves pleasure:
Now I want to live and die by the side of my spouse—
in this life as in the others, in him alone I seek refuge.

38. The intercalary month[18] is the most fruitful of all :
in it all the virtues of the six seasons are contained—

17. Here "Dharma" refers to the rule of the Jaina monks and nuns, which consists in a life of total continence and hard penance.

18. An "extra-month" is introduced in the Hindu lunar calendar every third year, to make up for the missing days so as to make the lunar calendar approximatively coincide with the solar year. The month which is so "doubled" is usually the month of Āshāḍh, the first month of the rains. Ths extra-month is considered particularly holy and a propitious time for extra vows (vratas) and devotions.

Eager to go and join her Beloved
Ugrasen's daughter has taken leave of all.

39. Followed by her five friends and all her attendants
for the love of her spouse, Rājal departed for Girnār :
There, together with all her friends, the heroic Rājal
took initiation from her Lord [Nemi].

For the love of prince Nemi, at Girnār
The princess Rājal turned a *Siddhī* !

नेमिनाथ-चतुष्पदिका

सोहग-सुंदर घण-लायण्णु सुमरवि सामिउ सामल-वन्नु ।
सखि-पति राजल-चडिउत्तरिय बारमास सुणि जिम वज्जरिय ॥१॥

नेमि-कुमरु सुमरवि गिरनारि
सिद्धी राजल-कन्न कुमारि ॥ (आंकिणी)

'श्रावणि सरवणि कडुयं मेहु गज्जइ, बिरहि रि! झिज्झइ देहु ।
विज्जु झवक्कइ रक्खसि जेव नेमिहि विणु, सहि! सहियइ केम?'॥ २ ॥

सखी भणइ 'समिणि! मन झुरी दुज्जण-तणा म वंछित पूरि ।
गयउ नेमि, तउ विणठउ काइ अछइ अनेरा बरह सयाइ' ॥ ३ ॥

बोलइ राजल इहु वयणु 'नत्थी नेमि-समं वर-रयणु ।
धरइ तेजु गह-गण सवि ताब गयणि न उग्गइ दिणयरु जाव' ॥४॥

भाद्रवि भरिया सर पिक्खेवि स-करुण रोअइ राजदेवि ।
'हा! एकलडी मइ निरधार किम ऊवेखिसि, करुणा-सार?'॥५

भणइ सखी'राजल! मन रोइ नीठुरु नेमि न अप्पणु होइ ।
सिंचिय तरुवर परि पलवंति गिरिवर पुण कड(?) डेरा हुंति' ॥६॥

'साचऊँ, सखि! वरि गिरि भिज्जंति किमइ न भिज्जइ सामल-कंति ।
घण बरिसंतइ सर फुट्टंति सायरु (?)पुणु घणु ओहडु(?) लिंति' ॥ ७ ॥

आसा मासह अंसु-प्रवाह राजल मिल्हइ विणु नमिनाह ।
'दहइ चंदु चंदण हिम-सीउ विणु भत्तारह सउ विवरीउ' ॥८॥

'सखि! न-वि खीना नेमिहि रेसि मन आपणपउँ तउँ खय नेसि ।
जिणि दिक्खाडिउ पहिलउँ छेहु न गणिउ अट्ठ-भवंतर-नेहु' ॥९॥

'नेमि दयालू, सखि! निरदोसु कीजइ उँग्रसिण-ऊपरि रोसु ।
पसुय (?) भराविउ मूकउ वाड़ु मुझ प्रिय-सरिसउ कियउ विहाडु'॥ १० ॥

कत्तिग क्षित्तिग ऊगइ संझ रजमति झिझि (?) उहुइ अति-झंझ ।
राति-दिवसु अछइ विलवन्त 'वलि वलि, दय करि दय करि, कंत!' ॥ ११ ॥

'नेमि-तर्णी, सखि! मूकि-न आस कायरु भग्गउ सो घर-वास ।
इमइ इसी सनेहल नारि जाइ कोइ छंडवि गिरनारि?'॥१२॥

'कायरु किम, सखि! नेमि-जिणंदु जिणि रिणि जित्तउ लक्खु नरिंदु ।
फुरइ सासु जा अग्गलि नास ताव न मिल्हउँ नेमिहि आस'॥१३

मगसिरि मग्गु पलोअइ बाल इण परि पभणइ नयण-विसाल ।
'जो मइ मेलइ नेमि-कुमार तसु णीवेल (?) वहउ सवि-वार' ॥ १४ ॥

'एहु कदाग्रहु तउ, सखि! मिल्हि करिसि काइ तिणि नेमिहि,हिल्लि ।
मंडि चडाविउ जो किर मालि "हे! हे! कुकरइ टोहण-कालि?' ॥ १५ ॥

'अठ भव सेविउ, सखि! मइ नेमि तमु ऊमाइउ किम न करेमि? ।
अवगन्नेसइ जइ मइ सामि लग्गी अछिसु तो-इ तसु नामि'॥१६

'पोसि रोस सवि छंडिवि, नाह! राखि राखि मइ मयणह पाह ।
पडइ सीउ, नवि रयणि विहाइ लहिय छिद्द सवि दुक्ख अमाइ' ॥ १७ ॥

' "नेमि! नेमि!" तु करती, मुद्धि! जुव्वणु जाइ न जाणिसि मुद्धि।
पुरिस-रयण-भरियउ संसारु परणि अनेरउ कुइ भत्तारु'
॥ १८ ॥

'भोली तउ, सखि! खरी गमारि वरि अच्छंतइ नेमि-कुमारि।
अन्नु पुरिसु कुइ अप्पणू नडइ? गइ(?) वरु लहिउ, कुरासभि
चडइ?' ॥ १९ ॥

माह मासि माचइ हिम-रासि देवि भणइ 'मइ, प्रिय! लइ पासि
तइ विणु, सामिय! दहइ तुसारु नव-नव-मारिहि मारइ मारु'
॥ २० ॥

'इहु, सखि! रोइसि सहु अरन्नि हत्थि कि जामइ धरणउ कन्नि? ।
तउ न पतीजसि, माहरि माइ! सिद्धि-रमणि-रत्तउ नेमि जाइ'
॥ २१ ॥

'कंति वसंतइ हियडा-माहि वाति पहींजउँ किम, हलसाइ
(?) ।
सिद्धि जाइ तउ काइ त बौह सरसी जाउ त उँग्रसेण-धीय' ॥२२

फागुण (?) वा-गुणि पन्न पडंति राजल-दुक्खि कि तरु रोयंति? ।
'गब्भि गलिवि हउँ काइ न मूय?' भणइ विहंगल धारणि-धूय ॥२३

'अजिउ भणिउ करि, सखि! विम्मासि अछइ भला वर नेमिहि पास(?) ।
अनु, सखि! मोदक जउ नवि हुंति छुहिय सुहाली कि न रुच्चंति?
॥ २४ ॥

'मणह पासि जइ वहिलउ होइ नेमिहि पासि ततलउ न कोइ ।
जइ, सखि! वरउँ त सामल-धीरु धण-विणु पियइ कि चातकु नीर?'
॥ २५ ॥

चैत्र मासि वणसइ पंगुरइ वणि वणि कोयल टहका करइ ।
पंचबाण करि धनुष धरेवि वेझइ मांडी राजल-देवि ॥ २६ ॥

जुइ, ससि! मातउ मासु वसंतु इणि खिलीज्जइ, जइ ह्ुइ कंतु ।
रमियइ नव नव करि सिणगारु लिज्जइ जीविय-जुब्बण-सारु' ।।२७

'सुणि, सखि! मानिउ मुझु परिणयणु नवि ऊवरि थिउ बैंधव-वयणु ।
जइ पडिवन्नइ चुकाइ नेमि जीविय जुव्वणु जलणि जलेमि' ।। २८

वइसाह ह विहसिय वण-राइ मयण-मित्तु मलयानिलु वाइ ।
'फुट्टि, रि हियडा! 'माझि वसंतु विलवइ राजल पिक्खिउ कंतु ।।२६।।

सखी दुक्ख वीसरिवा भणइ 'सभलि, भलरउ किम रुणझूणइः ।
"दीस पंच थिरु जोध्वणु होइ खाउ, पियउ, विलसउ सहुकोइ'' '
।। ३० ।।

रमणि पसंसइ राजल-कन्न 'जीह कंतु वसि, ते पर धन्न ।
जसु प्रिउ न करइ किमइ मुहाडि सा हउँ इक्क ज भुंड-निलाडि'
।। ३१ ।।

जिट्ठ(?) विरहु जिम तप्पइ सूरु 'धण-विओगि सुसियं नइ पूरु ।
पिक्खिउ फुल्लिउ चंपइ(?)-विल्ली राजल मूछीं नेह गहिल्लि ।।३२

'मुछी राणी' हा सखि! धाउँ(?) पढियउ खंडइ (?) जेवडु घाउ ।
हरिय मूछ चंदण-पत्रणेहिँ सखि आसासइ प्रिय-वयणेहिँ
।। ३३ ।।

भणइ देवि 'विरती संसार पडिखि पडिखि मइ?,जादव-सार! ।
निय-पडिवन्नउँ, प्रभु! संभारि मइ लइ सरिसी गढि गिरिनारि'
।। ३४ ।।

आसाढह दिढु हियउँ करेवि गज्जु विज्जु सवि अवगन्नेवि ।
भणइ वयणु उँग्रसेणह जाय 'करिसु धम्मु, सेविसु प्रिय-पाय'
।। ३५ ।।

मिलिउ सखी राजल पभणंति 'चिणय जेम न मिरीय खज्जंति ।
अउगी अच्छि, सखि! झखि मन आल तपु दोहिल्लउ, तउँ सुकुमाल'।।३६।।

'अठ भव विलसिउ प्रियह पसाइ किमइ जीवु, सखि! सुख[ह]न थाइ ।
हिव प्रिय-सरिसउँ जीविय-मरणु इण भवि पर-भवि निमि जु सरणु' ॥ ३७ ॥

अधिकु मासु सवि मासहि फिरइ छह-रितु-केरा गुण अणुहरइ ।
मिलिवा प्रिय ऊबाहुलि हूय सउ मुकळाविउ उँग्रसेण-धूय ॥३८॥
पंच सखी-सइ (?) जसु परिवारि प्रिय-ऊमाही गइ गिरिनारि ।
सखी-सहित राजल गुण-रासि लेइ दिक्ख परमेसर-पासि ॥ ३९ ॥

निम्मल केवल-नाणु लहेंवि सिद्धी सामिणि राजल-देवि ।
रयणसिंह-सूॅरि पणमवि पाय बार-इ मास भणिया मइ, भाय! ॥ ४० ॥

नेमि-कुमारु सुमरवि गिरनारि ।
सिद्धि राज-कन्न कुमारि ॥

(ed. H.C. Bhayani, *Srī Forbes Gujarāti Sabhā Granthāvalī*, Bombay 1955)

VIII

JINAPADMA SŪRI

SHRĪ STHŪLIBHADRA PHĀGU [old Gujarātī]

Bowing down to the feet of Pārshvajinendra[1]
and having invoked Sarasvatī,
I shall sing the virtues of Sthūlibhadra,
the best of ascetics, in the form of a Phāgu.[2]

[Bhāsa 1]

Fortunate, handsome, a storehouse of virtues was he,
With his complexion brilliant as gold, he was as a necklace
on the neck of Dame Continence[3] herself.
That king of ascetics, Sthūlibhadra, in the course of his
wanderings,
One day reached the city of Pātaliputra.

During the four months of the rainy season, the holy men,
joyful,
Go and take the *abhigraha*[4] from their guru, the virtuous
men :
On the order of his guru, Arya Vijaya Sambhūti Sūri,
therefore,
The great ascetic Sthūlibhadra went to the house of the
courtesan Kosā.

1. Pārshvanātha one of the Jinas or Tīrthānkaras.
2. About the literary phāgu form, cf. Supra, pp. 18-25
3. *sanjamā-sirī*, lit. "Shrī (goddess Lakshmī) in the form of "Continence or restrain."
4. *abhiggaha* (*ābhigraha*) is a particular vow of austerity which is taken by the Jaina monks at the beginning of the rainy season on their guru's injonction.

Seeing the great ascetic at the door of her house,
Kosā was stirred : hastily she sent a servant to welcome him,
Then, all in a flutter, her necklace dangling on her breast,
The courtesan Kosā herself went to meet the great ascetic,
with joined palms.

The ascetic wished her : "May you obtain the Dharma!"
Then he went straight to the visitors' hall[5] :
There he took his residence,
his heart firm and dauntless like that of a young lion.

Bhāsa 2

Jhirimiri, jhirimiri, jhirimiri, clouds are pouring rain,
Khalahale, khalahala, khalahala, rivers flow rapidly,
Jhabajhaba, jhabajhaba, jhabajhaba, flashes of lightning,
Tharahara, tharahara, tharahara, the Virahinī trembles!

While the clouds issue deep and melodious rumblings,
The god-with-the-five-arrows[6] prepares his flower-weapons—
While the Ketakī-flowers spread their fragrance
The lovers placate their beloved, clasping their feet.

While a soft, cool and fragrant breeze is blowing,
The pride of haughty belles goes to naught—
While the rain-heavy rain-clouds gather in the yard of the sky,
Tears well up and shine in the eyes of far-way travellers.

When, excited by the rumbling of the clouds,
the peacocks begin to dance,
Then the haughty women are abashed,
like thieves taken red-handed!

Bhāsa 3

Then the courtesan, all in a flutter adorns herself,
Smearing her body with precious ointments of many hues—

5. Chitrashālā, "a hall decorated with paintings" : it is a visitor's hall, separated from the private appartments.

6. The god of love, Kām or Madan, see Glossary : *Kām*.

With Champak, Ketakī and Jaī flowers,[7] she decorates her head
And she drapes herself in delicate, exquisite clothes.

Lahalaha, *lahalaha*, *lahalaha*, pearls rustle on her breast,
Ranarana, *ranarana*, *ranarana*, ring her anklets,
Jhagamaga, *jhagamaga*, *jhagamaga*, twinkle her earrings,
Jhalahala, *jhalahala*, *jhalahala*, sparkle all her jewels!

Her braid of hair glistens like Madan's own sword,
The dark line of hair on her waist is straight and beautiful,[8]
Her high breasts are enticing like love-bouquets,
As two jars of nectar placed there by Love itself!

She applies collyrium an her eyes
and on the parting of her hair
And the cups of her bosom she covers
with a half-open bodice.

Bhāsa 4

Her ears oscillate like the swing of Madan,
Her eyes are ever in motion like pretty wavelets,[9]
Her cheeks are full like small round cushions,
Her tender, pure throat sounds like the voice of the conch,

Her navel is a well full of Beauty's nectar,
Her thighs look like Madan's twin pillars
Her nails resemble flower-buds—sharp as Kāmdev's goad—
And the bells tied at her lotus feet tinkle : *rimijhimi*, *rimijhimi* !

7. These are flowers of the rainy season, celebrated for their fragrance.

8. A thin line of hair above the navel, visible between the bodice and the petticoat is considered as very attractive.

9. The courtesan Kosā, like all the dancing-girls, practices the art of gracefully moving her neck and ears as well as her eyes.

Her whole body is in the bloom of youth, inebriated with new love,
Spreading waves of perfume, like the first love-game of Rati[10],
With lips red as the Bimba fruit and the complexion of the Champak flower,
She is a feast for the eyes— of infinite charm and grace.

In that splendid attire
when Kosā went to meet the ascetic,
Then all the gods and gandharvas
gathered in the sky to gaze at her.

Bhāsa 5

The young woman throws oblique, alluring glances at him.
Accompanied by provoking mimic and gestures—
But the ascetic remains unmoved—then she adresses him so :
"O my Lord ! The pain of separation I endure for you scorches my body as a flame !

Why do you reject a love of twelve years ?
Why do you show me such cruelty ? "
Replies Sthūlibhadra : "O you, Harlot, why do you take so much trouble ?
Iron-armoured is my heart and your words cannot pierce it ! "

"O Lord, I pine for you ! Show me some tenderness
And spend this rainy season with me !"
Replies the ascetic : "O you, Harlot, I am married to a beautiful Siddhī :[11]
I've given my heart to Dame Continence[12], to her alone shall I make love."

10. Rati, the Passion, is Kām (Modan)'s wife.

11. Cp. *supra*, RĀJAL-BĀRAHMĀSĀ, n. 1; here the beautiful "Siddhī" is not a Jaina nun, but the personification of the Jaina monk's ideal of chastity.

12. Cf. *supra* n. 3.

Replies Kosā : "True indeed is the proverb which says
"Men are fond of novelties"—
See now that King of ascetics drops me
to enjoy himself with a "Dame Continence" ! "

Bhāsa 6

The Prince of ascetics, full of the liquor[13] of Self-restrain, tells Kosā :
"Who would drop the Jewel-of-desire and exchange it for a mere stone ?
Why would give up Dame Continence, suffused with the light of Dharma,[14]
To embrace you, O Kosā ?"

Says Kosā : "First gather the fruit of your youth
And then you'll dally with your Dame Continence !"
Replied the ascetic : "What I have chosen, I have chosen :
Who in this world could now lead my soul astray ?"

In such way did the perfect ascetic Sthūlibhadra
repel the enticement of Kosā :
She wondered at the firmness of his soul—
deeply moved, she rejoiced in her heart.[15]

Bhāsa 7

Heroic was that one who, by means of Knowledge, resisted the supreme temptation,
He who with the sword of Meditation knocked down Madan on the battle-field.
The gods rained down flowers, shouting cries of "Victory!":

12. *rasa*, "juice", "nectar" also means pleasure, especially sexual enjoyment—hence the antithesis : Sthūlibhadra "marries" Chastity and "enjoys" Self-restrain.

13. This Dharma is the Jaina religion or discipline.

14. The heroism of Sthūlibhadra brings about Kosā's conversion.

"Blessed, blessed be that Sthūlibhadra, who has defeated
Māra !"[16]

After imparting instruction to Kosā and completing his
chaumāsa[17],

The great sage, having kept his sacred vow, went back to
his Guru.

The Sūri praised him saying : "Yours indeed was the greatest
tour-de-force

Your glory will shine like the divine Conch,[18] gods and men
will bow before you !"

May this *phāgu* composed by Jinapadma Sūri
of the Kharatara order,[19] be pleasing to all :
And may it be sung and danced
in the month Chaitra, in great joy ![20]

16. Cf. *Supra* VIII, NEMINĀTHA-CHATUSPADIKĀ, n. 6.

17. *chaumāsa* takes the meaning of "period of special penance" in the Buddhist and Jaina context; cf. n. 4, *supra.*

18. A precious conch (*śankha*) is enumerated among the "nine treasures' of Kubera, the god of wealth. Sthūlibhadra is here compared to this divine, most effulgent *śankha.*

19. The *kharatara gaccha* is one of the "branches of the Shvetāmbara Jaina order, to which Sthūlibhadra belonged.

20. In the conclusion, the relation of the Phāgu songs and dances to the season of spring is maintained, in spite of the fact that the temptation of Sthūlibhadra and his heroic resistance take place in the rainy season : here the Chaumāsā song coincides with the Phāgu literary form, cf. pp. 22-25.

पणमिय पास-जिणिंद-पय अनु सरसइ समरेवी ।
थूलिभद्द-मुणिवइ भणिमु फाग-बंधि गुण के वी ।। १ ।।

(प्रथम मास)

(अह) सोहग-सुंदर रूववंतु गुण-मणि-भंडारो
कंचण जिम झलकंत-कंति संजम-सिरि-हारो ।
थूलिभद्द मुणि-राउ जाम महियलि बोहंतउ
नयरराय-पाडलिय-माहि पहुतउ विहरंतउ ।। २ ।।

वरिसालइ चउमास-माहि साहू गहगहिया ।
लियइ अभिग्गह गुरुह पासि निय-गुण-महमहिया ।
अज्ज-विजयसंभूइ-सूरि गुरु-वर मोकलावइ
तसु आएसि मुणीस कोस-वेसा धरि आवइ ।। ३ ।।

मंदिर-तोरणि आवियउ मुणिवरु पिक्खेवी
चमकिय चित्तिहि दासडिय वेगि जाइ वधावी ।।
वेसा अतिहि ऊतावलिय हारिहिं लहकंती
आविय मुणिवर-राय-पासि करयल जोडंती ।। ४ ।।
'धम्म-लाभु' मुणिवइ भणवि चित्रसालीँ मंगेवीँ ।
रहियउ सीह-किसोर जिम धीरिम हियउ धरेवीँ ।। ५ ।।

(द्वितीय भास)

झिरिमिरि झिरिमिरि झिरिमिरि ए मेहा वरिसंते
खलहल खलहल खलहल ए वाहला वहंते ।।

झबझब झबझब झबझब ए वीजुलिय झवक्कइ
थरहर थरहर थरहर ए विरहिणी-मणु कंपइ ।। ६ ।।

महुर-गँभीर-सरेण मेह जिम जिम गाजंते
पंचबाण निय-कुसुम-वाण तिम तिम साजंते ।।
जिम जिम केतकि महमहंत परिमल विहसावइ
तिम तिम कामिय चरण लग्गि निय-रमणि मनावइ ।। ७ ।।

सीयल कोमल सुरहि वाय जिम जिम वायंते
मान-मडप्फर माणिय तिम तिम नासंते
जिम जिम जल-भर-भरिय मेह गयणंगणि मिलिया
तिम तिम पंथिय-तणा नयण नीरिहिँ झलहलिया ।। ८ ।।

मेहा-रव-भर ऊलटि य जिम जिम नाचइ मोर ।
तिम तिम मणिणि खलभलइ साहीता जिम चोर ।। ९ ।।

[तृतीय भास]

अह सिंगारु करेइ वेस मोटइ मन-ऊलटि
रइय(?) अंगि बहुरंगि चंगि चंदण-रसऊगटि ।।
चंपक-केतिक-जाइ-कुसुम सिरि खुँप भरेई
अति-अच्छउ सुकुमाल चीरु पहिरणि पहिरेइ ।। १० ।।

लहलह-लहलह-लहलह ए उरि मोतिय-हारो
रणरण-रणरण-रणरण ए पगि नेउर-सारो ।।
झगमग-झगमग-झगमग ए कानिहिँ वर-कुंडल
झलहल-झलहल-झलहल व आभरणहँ मंडल ।। ११ ।।

मयण-खग्गु जिम लहलहए जसु वेणी-दंडो
सरलउ तरलउ सामलउ(?) रोमावलि-दंडो ।।
तुंग पयोहर उल्लसइ [जिम] सिँगार थवक्का
कुसुम-बाणि निय अमिय-कुंभ किर थापणि मुक्का ।।१२।।

कज्जलि अंजिवि नयण-जुय सिरि सइँथउ फाडेईँ ।
वोरीँ यॉवडि-कंचुलिय पुण उर-मंडलि ताडेइ । १३ ।।

[चतुर्थ भास]

कन्न-जुयल जसु लहलहंत किर मयण-हिंडोला
चंचल चपल तरंग-चंग जमु नयण-कचोला ।।
सोहइ जासु कपोल-पालि जणु गालिमसूरा
कोमल विमलु सुकंठु जासु वाजइ सँख-तूरा ।। १४ ।।

लवणिम-रस-भर-कूवडिय जसु नाहिय रेहइ
मयण-राय किर विजय-खंभ जसु ऊरू सोहइ ।।
जसु नह-पल्लव कामंदेव-अंकुस जिम राजइ
रिमिझिमि रिमिझिमि रिमिझिमि पाय कमलि घाघरि यसु
वाजइ ।।१५।।

नव-जोवण-विलसंत-देह नव-नेह-गहिल्ली
परिमल-लहरिहि महंमहंत रइ-केलि पहिल्ली ।।
अहर-बिब पखाल-खंड वर-चंपा-वन्नी
नयण-सलूणीयँ हाव-भाव-बहुरस-संपुन्नी ।। १६ ।।

इथ सिंगार करेवि वर जउ आवी मुणि-पासि ।
जोएव कउतिगि मिलिय सुर-किन्नर आकासि ।। १७ ।।

[पंचम भास]

(अह) नयण-कडक्खिहिँ आहणए वांकउ जोवंतीं
हाव-भाव-सिगार-भंगि नवं-नविय करंति ।।
तह वि न भीजइ मुणि-पवरोँ तउ वेस बौलावइ
'तवण तुल्लु तुह विरह, नाह ! माह तणु संतावइ' ।।१८।।

बारहँ वरिसहँ तणउ नेहु किणि कारणि छंडिउ
एवडु निट्ठुरमणउँ काइँ मू-सिँउ तुँम्हि मंडिउ ।।

थूलिभद्द पभणेइ 'वेस ! अइ-खेदु न कीजइ
लोहिहि घडियउ हियक मज्झ, तुह वयणि न भीजइ' ॥ १९॥

'मह विलवंतिय-उवरि, नाह ! अणुराग धरीजइ
एरिसु पावस-कालू सयलु भू-सिँउ माणीज़इ' ॥
मुणिवइ जंपइ 'वेस! सिद्धि-रमणीं परिणेवा
मणु लीणउ सजम-सिरीँहिँ सिउँ भोग रमेवा' ॥ २० ॥

भणइ कोस 'साचउँ कियउँ "नवलइ राचइ लोउ"।
मू मिलिहिवि संजम-सिरिहँ जउ रातउ मुणि-राउ' ॥२१॥

[षष्ठ भास]

उवसम-रस-भर-पूरिय यउ(?) रिसि-राउ भणेइ
'चिंतामणि परिहरवि कवणु पत्थरु गिह्णेइ ॥
तिम संजम-सिरि परिचएवि बहु-धम्म-समुज्जल
आलिंगइ तुह, कोस! कवणु पसरंत-महाबल' ॥ २२ ॥

'पहिलउ हिवडाँ कोस कहइ 'जुव्वण-फलु लीजइ
तयणंतरु संजम-सिरीँहिँ सुहिण रमींजइ' ॥
मुणि बोलइ 'जं मइँ लियउ तं लियउ ज होइ(?)
कवणु सु अच्छइ भवण-तले जो ममहणु मोहए' ॥२३॥

इणि परि कोसा अवगणिय थूलिबद्द-मुणिराइ।
तसु धीरिम अवधारि-करि चमकिय चित्ति सुहाइ ॥२४॥

[सप्तम भास]

अइ-बलवंतु सु मोह-राउ जिणि नाणि निधाडिउ
झाण-खडग्गिण मयण-सुहड समरंगणि पाडिउ ॥
कुसुम-वुट्ठि सुर करइ तुट्ठ तह जयजय कारो
'धनु धनु एहु जु थूलिभद्दु जिणि जीतउ मारो' ॥ २५ ॥

पडिवोहिवि तह कोस वेस चउमासि अणंतरु
पालि अभिग्गह ललिय वलिय गुरु पासि मुणीसरु ॥
'दुक्कर-दुक्कर-कारगु' त्ति सूरिहिँ सु पसंसिउ
संख-समुज्जल-जस-लसंतु सुर-नरिहिँ नमंसिउ ॥ २६ ॥

नंदउ सो सिरि-थूलिभद्द जो जुगह पहाणो
मलियउ जिणि जगि मल्ल-सल्ल रइवल्लह-माणो ॥
खरतर-गॅच्छि जिणपदम-सूल्ल-किउ फागु रमेवउ
खेला-नाचइ चैत्र मासि रंगिहि गाएवउ ॥ २७ ॥

(ed. H. C. Bhayani, Śrī Forbes Gujarātī Sabhā Granthāvalī, 61 Bombay 1955)

GLOSSARY

Agahan The ninth month of the Hindu year, corresponding to November-December; also called *Mārga* q.v.

Āshāḍh (*āṣādha*) The fourth month of the Hindu year, corresponding to June-July; the first month of the rainy season.

Āshvin (*āśvina*) The seventh month of the Hindu year, corresponding to September-October; the last month of the rainy season; also called "Knwār" q.v.

badāyī (*baḍāyī*) Lit. "grandmother"; a respectful form of address to an elderly woman.

Baisākh (*vaiśākha*) The second month of the Hindu year, corresponding to April-May.

Basant (*vasanta*) The season of spring, spread over the two months of *Chaitra* and *Baisākh*, q.v. It is the season of flowering trees and love-play. "Basant" is often personified as an ally of the god of Love, Kām or Madan, q.v. "Playing Basant" refers to the dances of the season of spring, such as *charcharī*, *dhamāri* or *phāg* q.v.

Basant panchamī "The fifth day" in the bright half of the month of *Māgh*, q.v., is a feast celebrating the end of winter and heralding the coming of spring. From Basant Panchamī till the end of *Phālgun*, q.v., people sing songs on the erotic theme, know as *phāg* or *phāg* q.v.

Bhādra, *Bhādon* The sixth month of the Hindu year (August-September). It is the darkest month of the year.

bhaṁvar (*bhramara*) The Indian black-bee, which symbolizes the inconstant lover, hovering from flower to flower to drink their nectar. In folk-songs it also serves as a messenger between separate lovers.

Chaitra (*caitra*) The first month of the Hindu year, corresponding to March-April.

chakvā (*cakravāka*) The Chakvā is a water-bird (the ruddy goose). According to popular belief, the Chakvā and its female, the Chakvī, are unable to meet long as the night lasts and they suffer from the pain of separation (*virah*). Therefore the Chakvī, as a *virahiṇī* (q.v.) piteously moans throughout the night.

chātak (*cātaka*) Another water-bird, also known as "Papīhā", q.v. According to popular belief, the Chātak bird is endlessly pining for the rain-drop of Svāti, the tenth *nakshatra* q.v. and will not drink of any other water. His call is interped as "*piu kahaṁ*": "Where is my beloved?" Hence its name of "Papīhā".

charcharī, *chācar* (*carcarī*) Lit. "frolic" "revelry; the *Charcharī* as well as the *Dhamārī* and *Phāg* q.v. is a type of song on a particular rythm (*tāl*) accompanying frolicsome play of the early-spring season, v. *Phāgu*, *Phāg*.

Dasserā (*daśaharā*) "The tenth day" ending the autumnal *Navarātri* "nine Rights" festival in honour of the warlike goddess Durgā. The tenth day is dedicated to Durgā as "Vijayalakshmī," goddess of Victory.

dhāk (*dhākā*) The Ḍhak (*Butea frondosa*) is a thorny jungle tree usually associated to the Palāsh tree.

Dhamār, *dhamārī*) V. *Phāgu*, *Phāg*.

Dīvālī (*dīpāvalī*) The "Feast of Lamps" in honour of Lakshmī, goddess of wealth and good luck, is celebrated on the moonless day (*amāvasya*) of the month of Kārttik, q.v.

hamsa (*haṁsa*) The beautiful water-birds known as "hamsas" (the Brahmini duck) are supposed to have their permament dwelling on the inaccessible crystal-clear Mānsarovar lake, high up in the Himalayas.

Hanumān The divine monkey Hanumān, "son of the Wind" and endowed with enormous strength, appear as a faithful ally of prince Rāma in the *Rāmāyana* Epic. In order to find Sītā, Hanumān reaches the far-away city of Lankā, travelling through the air, and sets the whole city on fire.

Holī (*holikā*) "Holī or "Phāg" (q.v.) refers to the New-Year carnival, which begins with the lighting of the Holī bonfire on the full-moon-night (*pūrṇimā*) of the month of Phālgun (or Phāg), which is the last month of the Hindu year. The next day (Chaitra krishna 1) is the first day of the New Year.

Mutual aspersion with red powder (*gulāl*) and reddyed water, songs and dances, often of an obscene character, are part of the Holi festivities. Such songs and dances are called *charcharī*, *dhamāri* or simply *phāg*, q.v.

Jeṭh (*jyeṣṭha*) The third month of the Hindu-Year (May-June). It is the hottest month of the year.

jhūmāk Also called *jhūmār* : refers to a type of dance executed by women alone bending and swinging their torso. The *jhūmak* songs and dances are associated with several festival especially the Dīvālī festival.

Kailās (*kailāsa*) Name of the high himalayan peak which is said to be the abode of god Shiva.

Kājalī (From *kājal*, "lamp-black, collyrium") *kajalī* refers to a type of songs sung by women during the rainy season, especially on the feast known as *Kājalī Tīj*, q.v.

Kām (*kāma*) The god of Love, the Hindu Eros, also called "Madan" and "Pancham", q.v. Kām wields a bow a five flower-arrows to wound the lovers' heart, especially during the season of spring.

Kanhā v. *Krishna.*

Kārttik (*kārttika*) The eighth month of the Hindu year, corresponding to October-November.

Kunwar (*kumāra*) Another name of the month of Agahan, q.v.

koil (*kokila*) The Indian cuckoo, a black bird whose pathetic call is heard during the mating season. His cry is interpreted like that the *chātak* (q.v.) as an appeal of its "beloved". The black colour of its plumage is interpreted by poets as the result of having been scorched by "the fire of Virah".

Lankā, Palankā "Lankā", in the *Rāmāyaṇa* legend, is the name of the island citadel of the demon-king Rāvaṇa in the southern region, now identified with the island of Ceylon. As to "Palankā", it is an imaginary island situated even further than Lankā.

madan (*madana*) Lit. "He who maddens" (the lovers) is another name of Kām, q.v.

Māgh (*māgha*) The eleventh month of the Hindu year, corresponding to January-February.

Malaya A sweet-scented, cooling breeze supposed to blow from the Malaya mountain in South India, a famed hill covered with sandal-trees.

Mārga (*mārgaśīrṣa*) Another name for the month of "Agahan" q.v.

nakshatra (*nakṣatra*) Hindu astronomy knows of 28 *nakshatras* "asterisms" or Lunar mansions, beginning with *Shravishthā* (*śrāviṣṭha*) or Dhanishtha (*dhaniṣṭha*) and ending with *Shrāvana* (*śravaṇa*). The names of the twelve months are derived from the dominant corresponding asterism.

papīhā v. *chātak*.

paksha Lit. "wing", refers to each of the two parts of any month : the light *paksha* corresponds to the waking moon and the dark *paksha* to the waning moon.

Paush (*pauṣa*) The tenth month of the Hindu year, corresponding to December-January. It is the coldest month of the year.

pūjā The act of worship performed in honour a divinity. A simple *pūjā* normally includes the offering of appropriate flowers, leaves, fruit and incense. The *pūjā* offered to a deity is often preceded by a fast (*vrata*) in honour of the same deity.

phāgu, *phāg* (*phālguṇa*) A type of lyrical compositions, mostly on the erotic theme, associated with the early spring and the Holī carnival, also called "Phāgu" or "Phāg"; The dancing and play associated with the Holī carnival mostly are of an obscene character. See : *Holi*; *Phalgun*.

sāras (*sārasa*) A migratory bird, the Siberian crane; like the Chakvā's cry, the Sāras, cry is interpreted as a mournful call to its mate.

Shrāvan (*śravaṇa*) The fifth month of the Hindu year, corresponding to July-August.

Svāti The twentieth *nakshatra*. According to popular belief, the rain-drop of Svāti fulfils the ardent desire of the thirsty Chātak-bird, q.v. When the Svāti rain drop falls into open sea-shells, it produces pearls.

Tīj (*tīja*) *Tīj* means "third" : the feast of *Tīj* or *Tīj Kājalī* is a women's festival celebrated on the third day of the light *paksha* of Shrāvan. It is a feast in honor of Shiva and his consort Pārvatī and is of great importance to married women. On that day, they play and sing songs known as "kājalī" q.v. in honour of the goddess.

virah (*viraha*) Lit. "separation" : the pain of separation from a husband or lover; often personified in poetry.

virahinī (*virahiṇī*) A woman languishing in "the fire of Virah".

vrata A "vow" or religious observance, implying a fast in honour of a particular deity for the obtention of a boon. The *vrata* is usually coupled with a *pūjā* q.v.

Phālgu, *Phāgu*, *Phāg* The twelth and last month of the Hindu year, ending with the Holī festival, q.v.

BIBLIOGRAPHY

I. ENGLISH; FRENCH.

ARCHER, W. G., *Seasonal songs of the Patna district*, "Man in India", vol. XXII, 1952.

BROWN, N., *Vasanta-vilāsa, An Old Gujarātī Phāgu*, Bombay, 1942.

CHAUDHURI, J. B., *The Haṁsa-dūta of Vāmana Bhaṭṭa Bāṇa*, Calcutta, 1942.

DIVATIA, N. B., *Gujarati Language and Literature*, 2 vol., Bombay, 1932.

DUBEY, S. C., *Field Songs of Chattisgarh*, Lucknow, 1951.

FORBES, *Rās Mālā*, 2 vol., London, 1858.

GARCIN DE TASSY, *Histoire de la Litterature Hindouie et Hindoustanie*, 2 vol., Paris, 1947.

GHOSH, J. C., *Bengali Literature*, Oxford, 1948.

GRIERSON, G.A., *Some Biharī folk-songs*, JRAS, 1884, pp. 196 f.

GRIERSON, G. *Some Bhojpuri Folk Songs*, edition and translations, JRAS, 1886, pp. 207-26.

GROVER, C. E., *Folk Songs of Southern India* Madras 1871.

MISHRA JAYAKANTH, *Introduction to the folk-literature of Mithila*, Allahabad, 1950, 1951.

MITRA, S. C., I. *Bihari life in Bihari nursery rhymes*, Calcutta, 1963; II. *Santali life in Santali Folk Songs*, Bombay, 1924.

MUNSHI, K. M., *Gujarat and its Literature*, 2nd ed., Bombay, 1954.

SEN, D. C., *History of the Bengali Language and Literature*, Calcutta, 1911.

SEN, D. C., *Folk Literature of Bengal*, Calcutta University, 1920.

SEN, D. C., *Eastern Bengal Byllads of Mymensingh* (vol. I & II), Calcutta University, 1920.

SEN SUKUMAR, *History of Bengali Literature*, Calcutta, 1960.

TAWNEY, C. H., English translation of the *Prabandhacintāmaṇi* of Merutunga Ācarya, Calcutta, 1899.

TESSITORI, *Notes on the Grammar of the Old Western Rājasthānī with social references to Apabhraṁśa and to to Gujarātī and Mārvāṛī*, IA 1914, 1915, 1916.

TOD A. R., *Annals and Antiquities of Rajasthan*, repr. 2 vol., London 1957.

VAUDEVILLE, C., *A Note of the Ghatakarpara and the Meghadūta*, Proceedings of the All-India Oriental Conference, Twentienth session, Bhubhanesvar, 1959.

VAUDEVILLE C., *Dhola-Mārū-rā Dūhā, Une ancienne ballade du Rajasthan*, I. F. I. Pondichéry, 1962.

VAUDEVILLE, C. *Les Chansons des douze mois dans les litteratures Indoaryennes*, I.F.I., Pondichery, 1965.

VAUDEVILLE, C., *La conception de l'amour divin dans la Padmāvat de Muhammad Jāyasī, virah* et *'ishq*, JA, 1963, pp. 351.

VAUDEVILLE C., *Kabīr* I, Oxford, 1974.

VERRIER-ELWIN and HIVALE, *Folk Songs of the Maikal Hills*, Oxford University Press, Madras, 1944.

VERRIER-ELWIN, *Folk Songs of Chattisgarh*, Oxford University Press, Madras 1946.

ZBAVITEL, D., *The development of the Baromāsī in the Bengali Literature* Archiv Orientalni 29, 1961, pp. 583 f.

II. HINDI; BENGALI; GUJARATI.

BARTHWAL, P. *Gorakha-bānī*, 3rd. ed., Prayāg, V. S. 2017.

BHATTACHARYA, S. P., *Bhāratīya sāhitye baromāsyā*, Calcutta, 1920 (Bengali).

BHAYANI, H. C., ed. *Sthūlibhadra-phāgu* in "Śrī Forbes gujarātī sabhā granthāvalī", Bombay, V. S. 20II (with a translation in modern Gujarati).

CHATURVEDI, PARASHURAM, *Santa kāvya*, 2nd ed. Allahabad, 1961.

DALAL, O. D., ed. *Neminātha-phāgu* in "Pracīna-kāvya-sangraha", G. O. S. XIII; 2nd ed. in *Gurjārarāsāvali*, G. O. S. CXIII, Baroda, 1956.

DESAI, ed. *Neminātha-phāgu* in "Jaina yuga varṣa", 5, pp. 475 f.

DVIVEDI, H.H.N., ed. *Sādhana-kṛta Maināsat*, Gwalior, 1959.

GUPTA, M. P., ed. *Bīsaldev-rās*, Allahabad, 1953.

GUPTA, M. P., ed. *Candāyan*, Bombay, 1964.

GUPTA, P. L. ed. *Candāyan*, Bombay, 1964.

KAPADIA, H.R.R., *Phāgu-sāhitya* in "Jaina Satya Prakāśa", varṣa 11, ank 6.

NAHTA, Agarchand, *Sat saṁjñaka rācnaeṁ kī paraṁparā*, in "Rashṭabhāratī", May 1956.

NAHTA, Agarchand, *Bārahmāsa kī pracīna paraṁparā*, in Hindi Anuśīlan", varṣa 6, V. S. 2010, pp. 29 f.

NAHTA, Agarchand, *Rājasthān meṁ hindī ke hastalikhita granthoṁ kī khoja*, vol. IV, Udaipur, V.S. 1994, pp. 161 f.

NAMVAR SINGH, *Hindī ke vikāsa meṁ apabhraṁśa kā yoga*, Allahabad, 2nd ed. 1954.

RAY, Basantranjan, ed. *Srikṛṣṇakīrtana* (of Baḍu Chandīdās), Bāngīya Sāhitya, Pariṣad, Calcutta, 7th ed., 1961.

SANDESARA, B. J., ed. *Sthūlibhadra-phāgu* (of Jinapadmasūri) and *Neminātha-phāgū* of Rājaśekhara Surī, in "*Prācīna-phāgu-sangraha*, vol. II, 1952-53, Baroda, 1952, 1953.

SANDESARA, B. J. and PARKEH, S., *Pracīna-phāgu-sangraha*, University of Baroda, Baroda, 1955.

SINHA, D. P., *Bhojpurī loka-gīta meṁ karuṇa-rasa*, Allahabad, V. S. 2001.

SIRĪ GURU GRANTHA SĀHIB (nāgarī ed). Amritsar, 1951.

SURI, V. D., *Aitihāsika rāsa-sangraha*, Bhavnagar, 1917.

UPADHYAY, Krishnadev, *Bhojpuri lok-gīt*, Hindi Sahitya Sammelan, Allahabad vol. I : 1954, vol. II : 1956.

UPADHYAY, Krishnadev, *Lok-sāhitya kī bhūmikā*, Sahitya Bhavan Allahabad, 1957.

VAIDYA, B. M., *Rāsa-sāhitya*, Bombay, 1956 (with an Introduction by H. C. BHAYANI.)

VARMA, Satyajivan, ed. *Bīsaldev-rās*, Kashi, V. S. 1982.

INDEX